The Small Business

Digital Marketing

Playbook

ISBN: 9798876873729
Imprint: Independently published

1st edition 2024.

This publication is designed to provide accurate and authoritative information in regard of the subject matter covered within. It is sold with the understanding that the author is not engaged in rendering legal, accounting, or other professional services and any assistance or clarification sought on these matters should be sought from a competent professional.

"Life isn't about waiting for the storm to pass,

It's about learning to dance in the rain."

The Small Business Digital Marketing Playbook

1. Introduction

The Digital Age and Small Businesses

Why Digital Marketing is Crucial for Small Businesses

How this Book is Structured

The Path to Success

2. Understanding Your Small Business

Identifying Your Unique Selling Proposition (USP)

Target Audience Analysis

Setting Clear Business Goals and Objectives

3. Building a Strong Online Presence

Developing a Professional Website

    Choosing the Right Domain Name

    User-Friendly Design and Navigation

    Mobile Responsiveness

Content Strategy

    Creating High-Quality Content

    Blogging for SEO and Engagement

Social Media Profiles and Strategy

    Selecting the Right Platforms

    Content Posting Schedule

    Engaging with Followers

4. Search Engine Optimisation (SEO)

On-Page SEO

      Keyword Research and Optimisation

      Meta Tags and Descriptions

      Header Tags and Content Structure

Off-Page SEO

      Building High-Quality Backlinks

      Online Reputation Management

Local SEO for Small Businesses

      Google My Business Optimisation

      Local Citations and Reviews

5. Pay-Per-Click Advertising (PPC)

The Role of PPC Advertising

Setting Up Google Ads Campaigns

Budgeting and Bidding Strategies

Monitoring and Optimising PPC Campaigns

6. Email Marketing

Building and Managing an Email List

Crafting Effective Email Campaigns

Automation and Segmentation for Small Businesses

7. Social Media Marketing

Creating a Social Media Content Calendar

Paid Advertising on Social Platforms

13. Conclusion

Key Takeaways

Encouragement for Small Business Owners

Final Thoughts on Achieving Digital Marketing Success

1. Introduction

Welcome to The Small Business Digital Marketing Playbook. Having worked in and owned a number of small businesses over the years, I had lots of experience in being the person who needed to "sort marketing" and with a little intuition and research I managed to do pretty well. It wasn't until recently that I realised I really enjoyed the marketing side of things and set to studying marketing in earnest. I recently launched a small social media marketing agency and finally got myself on board with TikTok (I think in all honesty I'd been a little scared of it), and it didn't take long for me to realise its huge potential for small businesses.

Having lived the small business journey, I wanted to write this book to help others on that road. Of course, outsourcing to an agency is a great move, but sometimes there are good reasons to look after your marketing in-house – and it doesn't have to be so difficult. I hope to provide you with the knowledge and tools to be able to do as much as you need to successfully.

Small business accounts for the largest share of our economy, let's succeed together!

The Digital Age and Small Businesses

In today's fast-paced digital age, the landscape of business has undergone a profound transformation. The rise of the internet and the ubiquity of smartphones have reshaped the way we shop, interact, and make decisions. Small businesses have had to adapt quickly to this evolving environment, where traditional advertising methods are no longer sufficient to reach and engage with their target audiences. In the last eighteen months, generative AI has introduced a whole new dynamic to the opportunities and challenges that face small businesses, with the vast majority of businesses yet to leverage the possibilities. I should add at this point that I have used AI to help me create this book – there are times when writers block kicks in and to effectively communicate my thoughts, I have asked ChatGPT to help me reword or expand on topics so that they flow well and are easy for you to read, but the bulk of the work is my own and I hope you enjoy it!

Welcome to "The Small Biz Digital Marketing Playbook," a comprehensive guide designed to equip small business owners with the knowledge and strategies needed to thrive in the digital realm. In the pages that follow, we will embark on a journey to explore the intricacies of digital marketing and how it can be harnessed as a powerful tool for your small business.

This book serves as a comprehensive guide to help small business owners understand and implement effective digital marketing strategies to grow their businesses in the digital age. Each chapter will delve into practical tips, case studies, and actionable advice to ensure small business digital marketing success.

Why Digital Marketing is Crucial for Small Businesses

The emergence of digital marketing as an essential component of business success is not merely a trend; it is a fundamental shift that affects businesses of all sizes.

For small businesses, in particular, digital marketing offers a unique advantage. It provides a cost-effective means to reach a global or local audience, establish a strong online presence, and compete with larger players in the market. This breaks the barriers of traditional marketing which are typically higher cost and more difficult to measure.

However, the digital world can be overwhelming. The myriad of platforms, strategies, and tools can leave many small business owners feeling lost and unsure about where to begin. That's where this book comes in. I have carefully crafted this guide to provide you with a structured path to navigate the complex world of digital marketing.

In my own businesses I have previously engaged with digital marketing and had some great successes as a novice, and when I found I didn't have enough time to keep up the momentum I outsourced to lead generation consultants and social media agencies. It was later that I reignited my interest in digital marketing and studied it in depth before starting my own marketing agency.

It is essential that you consider digital marketing from two key angles: creative and data-driven. By doing this you will achieve maximum engagement from your visuals, and a deep understanding of you customers, which campaigns are effective and what it all means for your finances.

How this Book is Structured

This book is not a one-size-fits-all solution but rather a roadmap tailored to the unique needs of small businesses. It recognises the challenges that small businesses face, such as limited budgets and resources, and offers practical, budget-friendly strategies to overcome these hurdles.

From building a strong online presence to harnessing the power of SEO, PPC advertising, email marketing, and social media, I will walk you through the steps needed to achieve digital marketing success.

"The Small Biz Digital Marketing Playbook" is organised into a series of chapters, each addressing a critical aspect of digital marketing. We'll start by helping you understand your business, identify your target audience, and set clear objectives. From there, we will dive into the specifics of building and optimising your online presence, including website development, content creation, and social media engagement.

As you progress through this book, you will gain insights into advanced topics such as SEO, pay-per-click advertising, email marketing, and data-driven decision making. We'll also explore customer loyalty and retention, sharing strategies to keep your existing customers coming back for more.

The book concludes with a glimpse into the future of digital marketing, helping you prepare for emerging trends and technologies that will continue to shape the business landscape.

The Path to Success

As a small business owner, you already possess the entrepreneurial spirit and drive that are essential for success. "The Small Biz Digital Marketing Playbook" is here to provide you with the knowledge and tools necessary to amplify that spirit and achieve your digital marketing goals.

Are you ready to embark on this journey to digital marketing success? Let's begin by understanding your business and the fundamentals of creating a strong online presence, setting the stage for a prosperous digital future.

Welcome to the world of small business digital marketing, where success is within your reach.

2. Understanding Your Small Business

In the ever-evolving world of digital marketing, understanding your small business is the foundational step toward achieving success. In this chapter we delve into the essential elements that set the stage for effective digital marketing strategies.

By the end of this chapter, you will have a clear grasp of your business's unique selling proposition, a deep understanding of your target audience, and well-defined goals and objectives.

Identifying Your Unique Selling Proposition (USP)

Your Unique Selling Proposition (USP) is what sets your small business apart from the competition. It's the reason why customers should choose your products or services over those of your competitors. Discovering and defining your USP is a pivotal step in your digital marketing journey. Here's how to do it:

Analyse Your Products or Services: Begin by thoroughly analysing what you offer. What makes your products or services unique? What value do they bring to your customers? Concentrate on the benefits and not on the features that your products or service bring for your customers – what problems do they solve?

In-depth analysis of your products or services is a foundational step in crafting a compelling marketing strategy. Beyond understanding the features, delve into the core benefits and unique value propositions that your offerings bring to customers. Consider the problems your products or services solve for your target audience and how they fulfil specific needs or desires. This customer-centric approach is crucial in articulating a message that resonates with your audience. By focusing on the tangible benefits and outcomes, you can create marketing content that speaks directly to the pain points or aspirations of your customers, establishing a more profound connection and differentiation in a competitive market. Additionally, understanding the emotional impact of your products or services on your customers allows you to craft a narrative that goes beyond functionality, fostering a more memorable and impactful brand perception.

Competitor Research: Study your competitors. Identify their strengths and weaknesses. This will help you understand where your business can excel. What do your competitors do particularly well and how to you compare? What areas are the not so good at – can you seize an opportunity to be better?

Competitor analysis is a strategic imperative in positioning your business for success. By studying your competitors, you gain valuable insights into the dynamics of your industry and identify areas where your business can thrive. Assess their strengths and understand what makes them successful, whether it's exceptional customer service, innovative products, or effective marketing strategies. Equally important is identifying their weaknesses. Analyse where they fall short in meeting customer needs or addressing market gaps. This analysis not only helps you avoid potential pitfalls but also reveals opportunities for differentiation and improvement. By capitalising on the areas where competitors may struggle, you can position your business as a superior alternative and tailor your value proposition to meet unmet needs in the market, setting the stage for a competitive advantage.

Customer Feedback: Collect and analyse customer feedback. What do your customers love about your offerings? What concerns or complaints do they have? How do your customers feel about their relationship with your business?

Customer feedback is an invaluable source of insights that can shape and refine your business strategy. Actively collect and analyse feedback from your customers to understand their perspectives on your products or services. Identify the aspects that resonate positively with them, whether it's the quality, customer service, or unique features. Equally crucial is addressing concerns and complaints, using them as constructive feedback for improvement. By actively listening to your customers, you not only demonstrate a commitment to their satisfaction but also gain a deeper understanding of their needs and expectations. Additionally, assess the overall sentiment of your customers towards your business. Positive feedback can be leveraged for testimonials and marketing, while negative feedback presents an opportunity to rectify issues and strengthen customer relationships. Regularly engaging with customer feedback fosters a customer-centric approach, allowing your business to adapt and evolve in alignment with the ever-changing preferences and expectations of your audience.

Defining Your USP: Based on your analysis, clearly define your USP. This could be exceptional quality, unbeatable prices, superior customer service, or any other attribute that sets you apart.

Defining your Unique Selling Proposition (USP) is a pivotal aspect of strategic positioning in the market. Your USP encapsulates the distinctive element that sets your business apart from competitors and resonates with your target audience. This could be grounded in exceptional product quality, unbeatable pricing, a superior level of customer service, or any other attribute that provides unique value to customers. Your USP serves as the core message that differentiates your brand in the minds of consumers. It not only communicates the reasons why customers should choose your products or services over alternatives but also establishes a memorable and compelling brand identity. Through a well-defined USP, you not only attract your target audience but also foster loyalty by consistently delivering on the promise that sets your business apart in a crowded marketplace.

Target Audience Analysis

To effectively market your products or services, you need a deep understanding of your target audience. Your audience's needs, preferences, and behaviours should inform your marketing strategies. Here's how to analyse your target audience:

Demographics: Demographics involve identifying specific characteristics of your target audience, such as age, gender, location, income level, and other demographic factors. Understanding these demographic details is essential for tailoring your products, services, and marketing messages to align with the preferences and needs of your ideal customers. This information allows you to create targeted campaigns that resonate with specific segments of your audience, optimising your marketing efforts for better engagement and conversion.

Psychographics: Psychographics delve into the psychological aspects of your audience, including their values, lifestyles, attitudes, and interests. This deeper understanding enables you to craft marketing messages that go beyond surface-level demographics. By exploring the motivations and aspirations of your audience, you can create content and campaigns that emotionally connect with them. This personalised approach helps build a stronger brand-customer relationship and fosters a sense of loyalty, as customers feel that your brand understands and aligns with their values and lifestyle choices.

Behavioural Data: Behavioural data involves analysing the online behaviour of your audience to gain insights into their preferences and actions. By understanding which websites they visit, social media platforms they engage with, and keywords they search for, you can tailor your digital marketing strategies accordingly. This data allows you to target your audience on platforms where they are most active, optimise your website for relevant keywords, and tailor content to align with their interests. Behavioural data is a powerful tool for creating personalised and effective digital marketing campaigns that are more likely to capture and retain the attention of your audience.

Customer Personas: Create customer personas, which are detailed profiles of your ideal customers. Personas can guide your marketing efforts. Be really specific – give them names and build them out as your individual ideal customer, really get to know everything you possibly can about your ideal customer – where do they work, who do they live with, what are their other interests? Use the information you have gather in the three points above and build the customer persona from there. This will help you to sell to their needs, wants and desires.

Setting Clear Business Goals and Objectives

Once you understand your business and target audience, it's time to set clear and achievable goals and objectives for your digital marketing efforts. Without well-defined goals, it's challenging to measure success and progress. Here's how to establish them:

SMART Goals: Use the SMART framework - Specific, Measurable, Achievable, Relevant, and Time-bound - to create your goals. For example, "Increase website traffic by 20% in the next six months."
- Specific – Increase website traffic
- Measurable – By 20%
- Achievable – Links to both the measurable and time-bound elements in this case: - - 20% over six months is achievable.
- Realistic – Again in this case 20% over six months is realistic whereas 20% over 1 month would not be.
- Time-bound – In the next six months

Key Performance Indicators (KPIs): Identify the key metrics that will help you track your progress. These could include website visits, conversion rates, email open rates, and more.

Short-term and Long-term Objectives: Distinguish between short-term and long-term goals. Short-term goals might focus on immediate improvements, while long-term objectives could involve sustainable growth.

Budget Allocation: Determine how much of your budget will be allocated to various marketing channels and campaigns.

Chapter Summary

Understanding your small business, identifying your USP, analysing your target audience, and setting clear goals lay the foundation for a successful digital marketing strategy. The insights gained here will inform your decisions throughout this journey.

In the following chapters, we'll explore practical steps to leverage this knowledge and create a compelling online presence that resonates with your audience and drives your business forward.

3. Building a Strong Online Presence

We live and work In a digital age where your business's online presence is the cornerstone of your marketing strategy. A strong online presence not only enhances your visibility but also fosters trust and credibility among your target audience. You may have heard of "know, like, trust". People will essentially buy from people the know, like and trust. Having a strong online presence gives your target audience the opportunity to get to know you, to decide if they like you and to build trust in you.

In this chapter we explore the foundational elements of establishing a robust online presence, including developing a professional website, crafting an effective content strategy, and maximising your impact on social media.

Developing a Professional Website

Choosing the Right Domain Name: Your website's domain name is your digital address. Select a domain that is easy to remember, relevant to your business, and reflects your brand. Learn how to register a domain and choose a hosting service that suits your needs.

Shorter domain names are often easier to remember but they also come at a higher price. Many build-your-own website services will offer domain name purchasing and hosting within your package and have very flexible and easy to use templates to help you set up your website, many are also now beginning to offer generative AI tools to help you build a more functional and optimised website.

You can secure your domain using any one of a number of providers such as IONOS, WIX, Go Daddy to name a few. If you are an e-commerce business you can secure your domain via your host eg Shopify – however be aware that they may charge a higher price and it is very simple to secure your domain in Go Daddy and connect it to your Shopify site, this can often save you money. Many of the domain hosts will also offer a relatively cost-effective simple website builder if you want to build your own site, and most of these now have built in AI assistance along with a wide variety of pretty good templates to build your site around – just be aware of your SEO when writing your own copy and page titles etc.

User-Friendly Design and Navigation: A user-friendly website is essential. Optimise the user experience with clear navigation, intuitive menus, and responsive design for mobile devices.

It is also important that your website has quick loading times and compatibility with various browsers for effective search engine optimisation, and more importantly to ensure users are able to easily engage with your content and have a positive experience.

Mobile Responsiveness: In an era dominated by smartphones, mobile responsiveness is no longer an option but a necessity for a successful digital presence. With a significant portion of internet users accessing websites through mobile devices, ensuring your website adapts seamlessly to various screen sizes and resolutions is paramount. A mobile-responsive website guarantees that users, regardless of the device they use, experience a consistent and user-friendly interface. This not only enhances user satisfaction but is also crucial for search engine optimisation, as search engines prioritise mobile-friendly websites in their rankings. Regularly testing and optimising your site's performance on mobile devices are essential steps in meeting the expectations of today's digitally connected audience.

Content Strategy

Creating High-Quality Content: High-quality, engaging content is the lifeblood of your online presence. So it's really important to understand the different types of content, such as blog posts, articles, videos, and infographics.

Blog Posts: Blog posts serve as the backbone of your digital marketing strategy, providing an avenue for in-depth exploration of topics relevant to your small business. A well-crafted blog post not only enhances your website's SEO but also engages your audience with valuable and shareable content. Whether it's diving into industry trends, sharing expert insights, or offering practical tips, blog posts establish your business as an authority in your niche, attracting and retaining your target audience.

Articles: Articles, similar to blog posts, play a pivotal role in establishing thought leadership and conveying comprehensive information. In the context of small business digital marketing, articles can cover in-depth analyses, case studies, or market trends. Drawing from the principles outlined in the book, articles provide an opportunity for businesses to showcase expertise, foster trust, and contribute valuable insights to their audience, ultimately enhancing their online presence and authority within their industry.

Videos: In the age of visual content, videos are an indispensable tool for small businesses aiming to connect with their audience in a dynamic and engaging way. Videos can include product demonstrations, behind-the-scenes glimpses, and expert interviews. Leveraging platforms like TikTok, YouTube or other social media channels, businesses can create compelling video content to strengthen their brand identity, drive engagement, and boost overall visibility in the digital space.

Infographics: Infographics serve as a visual storytelling medium that condenses complex information into easily digestible and visually appealing graphics. Infographics are powerful for simplifying data, statistics, or processes, making them ideal for conveying key messages in a concise manner. Small businesses can leverage infographics on their website, in blog posts, or across social media to enhance understanding, increase shareability, and solidify their position as an informative and user-friendly source within their industry.

It's also important to leverage your own originality and to maintain a consistent brand voice. This is crucial because in the vast digital landscape, where competition is fierce and information overload is common, establishing a unique and recognisable brand identity is key to standing out.

By infusing your digital marketing efforts with originality, you create a distinctive and memorable brand that resonates with your audience. Originality not only sets you apart from competitors but also fosters a sense of authenticity, building trust with your customers.

Consistency in brand voice across various channels reinforces this originality. A consistent brand voice ensures that your messaging, tone, and values remain uniform, whether a customer interacts with your website, social media, or email campaigns. This cohesion strengthens brand recall, enhances customer loyalty, and contributes to a cohesive brand narrative that customers can easily recognise and connect with. In essence, leveraging your own originality and maintaining a consistent brand voice are integral components of a successful digital marketing strategy that builds a strong, trustworthy, and memorable brand presence in the digital realm.

Blogging for SEO and Engagement: Blogging serves as a dynamic and strategic approach to bolstering both your website's SEO and audience engagement. To harness its full potential, start by identifying relevant topics that align with your business, industry trends, and the interests of your target audience.

Conduct thorough keyword research to discover the terms and phrases your audience is actively searching for. You can also research keywords on www.ubersuggest.com which is a great resource. This ensures that your blog content is not only engaging but also optimised for search engines, increasing the likelihood of your pages appearing in relevant search results.

Craft your blog posts with a focus on providing value, solving problems, and addressing the needs of your audience. If finding content ideas is a struggle, take a look at www.answerthepublic.com and see what questions people are asking around your niche and you can create content to answer these, meeting your perfect audience's needs.

This dual approach of SEO optimisation and audience-centric content creation not only boosts your website's visibility on search engines but also establishes your blog as a valuable resource, fostering stronger connections with your audience.

Social Media Profiles and Strategy

Selecting the Right Platforms: Not all social media platforms are suitable for every business, and trying to build a presence on all them will be exhausting so it is best to do some research and work out which platforms will benefit your business most – where will your target audience see you the most? Explore the most popular platforms, like Facebook, Twitter, Instagram, LinkedIn, and Pinterest. Assess which platforms align best with your audience and goals.

Content Posting Schedule: Consistency is key in social media. Establish a content posting schedule that ensures regular updates and engagement with your followers.

Creating a social media content schedule can be efficiently streamlined with the help of various tools designed to enhance organisation, scheduling, and analytics. Here are some tools that can significantly aid in this process:

Hootsuite:
- *Key Features:* Hootsuite is a comprehensive social media management platform that allows you to schedule posts across multiple platforms, track performance analytics, and manage interactions in one dashboard. It supports popular social media channels like Facebook, Twitter, Instagram, LinkedIn, and more.

Buffer:
- *Key Features:* Buffer simplifies social media scheduling by allowing you to plan and schedule posts for various platforms in advance. It provides analytics to track engagement and optimise posting times. Buffer is user-friendly and integrates with major social media networks.

CoSchedule:

- *Key Features:* CoSchedule offers a centralised calendar for managing blog and social media content. It allows you to schedule posts, collaborate with team members, and integrate with various platforms. The platform also offers a Headline Analyser to optimise your post titles.

Later:
- *Key Features:* Later is particularly useful for Instagram scheduling. It allows you to visually plan your feed, schedule posts, and analyse engagement. Later also supports other platforms like Facebook, Twitter, and Pinterest.

Sprout Social:
- *Key Features:* Sprout Social provides a unified platform for social media scheduling, monitoring, and analytics. It offers collaboration tools for teams, detailed analytics reports, and a Smart Inbox to manage social interactions efficiently.

Planoly:
- *Key Features:* Planoly specialises in Instagram scheduling and planning. It allows you to visually organise and schedule posts, provides analytics insights, and supports Instagram Stories scheduling.

Trello:
- *Key Features:* While not solely a social media tool, Trello is an excellent project management tool that can be adapted for content scheduling. Create boards, lists, and cards to organise and plan your social media content collaboratively.

TweetDeck:
- *Key Features:* TweetDeck is a Twitter-specific tool that provides a customisable dashboard for monitoring and scheduling tweets. It's particularly useful for managing multiple Twitter accounts and tracking relevant hashtags.

By incorporating these tools into your social media strategy, you can streamline your content creation and scheduling processes, ensuring a consistent and effective presence across various platforms. Choose the tool that aligns with your specific needs and integrates well with the social media channels you prioritise.

Engaging with Followers: Social media is a two-way street. Discover strategies for interacting with your audience, responding to comments, and handling feedback, both positive and negative. Building a community around your brand fosters trust and loyalty. Ensure that you engage with other users posts too, this raises your visibility and shows you are an active member of the social media community.

Chapter Summary

A strong online presence is more than just a website; it's a combination of a professional website, engaging content, and active social media profiles. As you implement the strategies outlined in this chapter, you'll be well on your way to creating a digital presence that captures the attention of your target audience and positions your small business for success.

In the following chapters, we will explore more specific digital marketing strategies, including search engine optimisation (SEO), pay-per-click advertising (PPC), email marketing, and social media marketing, all of which can contribute to strengthening your online presence and expanding your reach.

4. Search Engine Optimisation (SEO)

In the vast digital landscape, your business's visibility on search engines is vital. Search Engine Optimisation (SEO) is the practice of optimising your online presence to rank higher in search engine results, making it easier for your target audience to find you.

In this chapter we'll explore the fundamental aspects of SEO, from on-page optimisation to off-page strategies and local SEO.

On-Page SEO

Keyword Research and Optimisation: Uncover the importance of keyword research in SEO. Learn how to identify relevant keywords for your business and integrate them strategically into your website's content.

With the rising prevalence of voice-activated devices and virtual assistants, optimising for voice search has become a critical aspect of on-page SEO. Voice searches tend to be more conversational and question-oriented, requiring a shift in the optimisation approach. To optimise for voice search, consider the following:

Conversational Content: Craft content in a conversational tone that mirrors how users naturally speak. This aligns with the way people typically phrase voice queries.

FAQ Sections: Include an FAQ section on your pages, addressing common questions users might ask. This not only provides valuable information but also aligns with the structure of many voice search queries.

Local Optimisation: Since a significant portion of voice searches is local, ensure your on-page content is optimised for local SEO. This includes incorporating location-specific keywords and details.

Mobile Optimisation: Voice searches often occur on mobile devices, so prioritise mobile optimisation for your website. Ensure fast loading times, responsive design, and a user-friendly mobile experience.

Schema Markup: Implement schema markup to provide search engines with additional context about your content. This can help search engines better understand the relevance of your content to voice search queries.

Both long-tail keywords and optimising for voice search are integral components of on-page SEO. Long-tail keywords enhance the specificity and relevance of your content, catering to niche audiences, while optimising for voice search ensures your content is aligned with the natural language used in voice-activated queries. Incorporating both strategies enhances the overall visibility and accessibility of your content in the evolving landscape of search engine optimisation.

Meta Tags and Descriptions: Explore the significance of meta tags and meta descriptions in optimising your website for search engines. Understand how to craft compelling meta tags and descriptions that entice users to click on your search results.

> **Meta Tags:** Meta tags are HTML tags that provide metadata about a webpage. These tags do not appear on the actual webpage but are embedded in the HTML code. The most common types of meta tags are the meta title and meta description. The meta title (or title tag) is a concise and accurate title for a webpage, usually displayed as the clickable headline in search engine results. Meta tags also include other elements like meta keywords and meta robots, although the latter has become less significant in modern SEO as search engines now prioritise content relevance and quality.

> **Meta Descriptions:** A meta description is a brief summary or snippet of content that describes the content of a webpage. Similar to meta tags, meta descriptions are part of a webpage's HTML code but are often displayed as a brief preview in search engine results. The primary purpose of a meta description is to provide users with a concise overview of what they can expect on the webpage. Well-crafted meta descriptions not only inform users but also play a role in enticing them to click through to the webpage. Effective meta descriptions are clear, compelling, and relevant to the

content on the page, influencing the click-through rate from search engine results pages (SERPs).

Header Tags and Content Structure: Properly structuring your content is not only user-friendly but also SEO-friendly.

Header tags (H1, H2, H3, etc.) are HTML elements that help structure and organise content on a webpage. Leveraging header tags not only enhances the readability for users but also assists search engines in crawling and indexing your content more effectively.

H1 Tag - Main Heading: The H1 tag represents the main heading of your page and should concisely summarise the primary topic or purpose of the content. Ensure it is unique on each page and provides a clear overview of what the content is about. The H1 tag signals the overarching theme of your page to search engines.

H2 Tags - Subheadings: H2 tags are used for subheadings that fall under the main heading (H1). They break down the content into more specific sections. Each H2 tag should introduce a new topic or subtopic. This hierarchical structure helps search engines understand the relationships between different sections of your content.

H3 Tags - Subsections: H3 tags further subdivide the content under H2 headings, providing additional granularity. Like H2 tags, each H3 tag introduces a subsection or a more specific aspect of the H2 topic. This layered structure enhances both user experience and search engine understanding of the content's organisation.

Best Practices:

- Use header tags sequentially (H1, H2, H3) to maintain a logical and hierarchical structure.
- Incorporate target keywords naturally into your header tags, emphasising the relevance of your content to search engines.
- Keep your headers concise, descriptive, and reflective of the content they introduce.
- Ensure that your headers accurately represent the content beneath them, enhancing user experience and search engine trust.

By utilising header tags effectively, you create a well-organised and user-friendly structure for your content, making it easier for both readers and search engines to navigate and comprehend the information on your webpage. This structured approach contributes to improved SEO and a more favourable user experience.

Off-Page SEO

Building High-Quality Backlinks: Backlinks from reputable websites are a powerful ranking factor. Learn strategies to earn or build high-quality backlinks, here are a few of my suggestions:

> **Create High-Quality Content:** Craft valuable, informative, and engaging content that naturally attracts links. When your content is noteworthy, other websites and bloggers are more likely to link to it as a valuable resource.

> **Guest Blogging:** Contribute guest posts to authoritative websites in your industry. Ensure that your guest posts provide genuine value to the audience and include a link back to relevant content on your site.

> **Broken Link Building:** Identify broken links on reputable websites within your niche. Reach out to the website owner or administrator, inform them of the broken link, and suggest your content as a replacement.

> **Skyscraper Technique:** Find popular content in your industry and create something even more valuable. Reach out to websites that linked to the original content, letting them know about your improved version and suggesting they link to it instead.

> **Build Relationships:** Establish relationships with influencers, bloggers, and businesses in your industry. Networking can lead to natural link-building opportunities, such as collaboration, co-authored content, or mentions on their platforms.

> **Utilize Social Media:** Share your content on social media platforms to increase its visibility. When others discover and

find value in your content, they may link to it from their websites or share it with their audience.

Resource Pages and Directories: Identify authoritative resource pages or directories in your industry and request inclusion. Ensure that your website or content provides genuine value and relevance to the page's theme.

Haro (Help a Reporter Out): Participate in platforms like HARO where journalists and writers seek expert opinions for their articles. If your expertise aligns with a request, you may be cited and linked in their published content. But do be careful not to suggest to the reporter that your contribution is conditional to a backlink as this is poor etiquette and may well result in your contributions not be welcomed!

Create Infographics: Design visually appealing and informative infographics related to your industry. Infographics are highly shareable, and when others use them, they are likely to link back to your site.

Internal Linking: Ensure your website has a solid internal linking structure. Link relevant pages within your own site to improve navigation and distribute link equity effectively.

Edu and Gov Links: Acquiring backlinks from educational institutions (.edu) and government websites (.gov) can significantly boost your site's authority. Participate in relevant educational or governmental programs or provide resources that these sites may find valuable.

Remember, the key to successful link-building is to focus on quality over quantity. Build relationships, offer value, and aim for links from reputable sources within your industry. Regularly assess your backlink profile and disavow any low-quality or spammy links to maintain a healthy link profile.

The disavow process in SEO involves informing search engines that you do not want certain backlinks to be considered when assessing your website's ranking. This is typically done through the Google Disavow Links tool, provided by Google Search Console.

Online Reputation Management: Your online reputation significantly impacts SEO.

Monitor Online Mentions: Regularly monitor mentions of your brand across various online platforms, including social media, review sites, and forums. Set up Google Alerts or use social media monitoring tools to stay informed about what people are saying about your business. Address any negative comments or reviews promptly and professionally, demonstrating a commitment to customer satisfaction.

Encourage Positive Reviews: Actively encourage satisfied customers to leave positive reviews on review sites, Google My Business, and other relevant platforms. Positive reviews not only contribute to a favourable online reputation but can also influence search engine rankings. Responding to positive reviews with gratitude further strengthens your brand's positive image.

Optimise Social Media Presence: Maintain an active and positive presence on social media platforms. Share valuable content, engage with your audience, and address customer inquiries or concerns. Consistency in social media activity contributes to a positive brand perception, and search engines often consider social signals in their ranking algorithms.

Optimise Website Content: Ensure that the content on your website reflects your brand positively. This includes highlighting positive customer testimonials, showcasing awards or recognitions, and addressing any concerns or controversies transparently. Optimising your website content with positive and accurate information helps shape a positive narrative around your brand.

Remember, a positive online reputation not only influences the perception of your brand but can also impact search engine rankings. Search engines aim to deliver the most relevant and trustworthy results to users, and a positive online reputation contributes to the overall credibility of your business in the digital space. Regularly assess and adapt your online reputation management strategies to maintain a positive image and support your SEO efforts.

Local SEO for Small Businesses

Google My Business Optimisation: Optimising your Google My Business (GMB) profile is crucial for local businesses as it directly influences your visibility in local search results. Here are a few of my suggestions:

Claim Your Google My Business Listing: If you haven't claimed your Google My Business listing, start by going to the Google My Business website and following the steps to claim your business. Google will send you a verification code by mail, phone, or email to confirm your ownership.

Complete Your Business Information: Ensure that all your business information is accurate and complete. This includes your business name, address, phone number, website URL, business hours, and categories. Consistency is crucial, and the information should match what is displayed on your website and other online platforms.

Add Engaging Business Descriptions: Craft a compelling and informative business description. Highlight key aspects of your business, including services, products, and what makes your business unique. Use relevant keywords to improve the chances of appearing in local search results.

Upload High-Quality Images: Add high-quality images that showcase your business, including the exterior, interior, team members, and products or services. Visual content not only attracts potential customers but also contributes to a positive user experience.

Collect and Respond to Reviews: Encourage satisfied customers to leave positive reviews on your GMB profile. Respond promptly and professionally to all reviews, whether positive or negative. Engaging with reviews demonstrates your commitment to customer satisfaction and can positively impact your local search ranking.

Utilise Google Posts: Take advantage of Google Posts to share updates, promotions, events, or other relevant content directly on your GMB listing. This feature allows you to engage with your audience and keep them informed about your business.

Optimise for Local SEO Keywords: Incorporate local keywords naturally into your business description and posts. Think about the terms potential customers might use when searching for businesses like yours in your specific location. This optimisation enhances your visibility in local search results.

Regularly Update Information: Keep your GMB profile updated with any changes to your business information, such as new operating hours, address updates, or contact information changes. Regular updates contribute to the accuracy and reliability of your listing.

By optimising your Google My Business profile, you improve your chances of appearing in local search results, especially in Google Maps and the local pack. This is crucial for attracting nearby customers who are actively searching for products or services in your area. Regularly monitoring and updating your GMB profile ensures that your business information remains accurate and relevant.

Local Citations and Reviews: Citations from local directories and customer reviews play a pivotal role in local SEO.

Local Citations:

Utilise Online Directories: Ensure your business is listed accurately on popular online directories such as Yelp, Yellow

Pages, and local chamber of commerce websites. Consistency in your business name, address, and phone number across these platforms is crucial for building trustworthy citations.

Industry-Specific Directories: Identify and list your business on industry-specific directories relevant to your niche. These directories provide targeted visibility to potential customers interested in specific services or products.

Local Business Associations: Join local business associations or organisations and ensure your business information is listed on their websites. These associations often have online directories that can contribute to your local citations.

Positive Reviews:

Optimise Customer Experience: Provide excellent products and services to your customers. A positive customer experience is the foundation for encouraging positive reviews. Ensure your team is trained to offer outstanding customer service.

Request Reviews Proactively: Actively request satisfied customers to leave reviews on platforms like Google My Business, Yelp, or industry-specific review sites. Make the process easy by providing direct links or clear instructions on how to leave a review.

Incorporate Reviews in Customer Communications: Include requests for reviews in your post-purchase communications, invoices, or follow-up emails. Express your appreciation for their business and kindly ask them to share their feedback online.

Offer Incentives Responsibly: While offering incentives for reviews can be effective, be cautious and ensure compliance with platform guidelines. Some platforms strictly prohibit incentivised reviews, so focus on creating a positive experience that naturally encourages customers to share their feedback.

Engage with Local Influencers:

Collaborate with Local Bloggers or Influencers: Identify local bloggers or influencers within your industry. Offer them an opportunity to experience your products or services and encourage them to share their experience online. Their reviews and endorsements can significantly impact your local reputation.

Participate in Local Events: Sponsor or participate in local events to increase your visibility in the community. Engage with event organisers, local media, and influencers attending these events to build relationships that may result in positive mentions and reviews.

Optimise Your Website:

Create a Reviews Landing Page: Dedicate a section of your website to showcase customer testimonials and reviews. This not only provides social proof but also contributes to your online reputation. Link to this page in your communications to direct customers to leave reviews.

Use Schema Markup: Implement schema markup on your website to highlight customer reviews. This markup can enhance the appearance of your business in search engine results by showcasing star ratings, making your listing more attractive to potential customers.

By implementing these strategies, your business can establish a strong local online presence through consistent citations and positive reviews, ultimately enhancing your visibility and reputation within the local community.

Chapter Summary

Search Engine Optimisation is a dynamic and ever-evolving field. As you apply the principles of on-page and off-page SEO and optimise your online presence for local search, you'll see improvements in your website's search engine rankings. This, in turn, will enhance your visibility and bring your small business to the forefront of potential customers' searches.

In the upcoming chapters, we'll delve into more advanced digital marketing strategies, including Pay-Per-Click advertising, email marketing, and social media marketing, to complement your SEO efforts and drive more targeted traffic to your website.

5. Pay-Per-Click Advertising (PPC)

Pay-Per-Click (PPC) advertising is a powerful tool in your digital marketing arsenal. It allows you to reach your target audience through paid advertising on search engines and other platforms.

In this chapter, we'll work through the ins and outs of PPC advertising, from campaign setup to budgeting and optimisation.

The Role of PPC Advertising

Understanding PPC:

Pay-Per-Click (PPC) is an online advertising model where advertisers pay a fee each time their ad is clicked. It is a form of digital marketing in which advertisers bid on specific keywords relevant to their products or services, and their ads are displayed on search engine results pages (SERPs) or other online platforms. The term "pay-per-click" reflects the billing structure, meaning that advertisers are charged only when a user clicks on their ad. PPC campaigns are often managed through platforms like Google Ads, Bing Ads, or social media advertising platforms, providing advertisers with tools to set budgets, target specific audiences, and track the performance of their ads in real-time. This model allows businesses to drive targeted traffic to their websites, increase brand visibility, and achieve specific marketing objectives while maintaining control over their advertising expenses.

When it comes to Pay-Per-Click (PPC) advertising, exploring different platforms is essential for reaching a diverse audience. Google Ads and Bing Ads are two major players in the PPC landscape, each offering unique advantages. Here's an expanded view of exploring these PPC platforms:

Google Ads:
- **Global Reach:** Google Ads is the largest and most widely used PPC platform, providing unparalleled reach. With billions of searches conducted on Google daily, advertisers can access a massive and diverse audience worldwide.
- **Keyword Targeting:** Google Ads offers robust keyword targeting capabilities, allowing advertisers to bid on specific keywords relevant to their products or services. Advertisers can use various keyword match types to refine their targeting.

- **Ad Formats:** Google Ads supports various ad formats, including text ads, display ads, video ads, and app promotion ads. This versatility enables advertisers to choose the format that best suits their marketing goals.
- **Audience Targeting:** Beyond keyword targeting, Google Ads provides sophisticated audience targeting options. Advertisers can target audiences based on demographics, interests, behaviours, and even website interactions through remarketing.
- **Shopping Ads:** For e-commerce businesses, Google Ads offers Shopping Ads, allowing advertisers to showcase products directly in search results with images, prices, and details.

Bing Ads:
- **Microsoft Search Network:** Bing Ads powers search advertising on the Microsoft Search Network, which includes Bing, Yahoo, AOL, and other partner sites. While Bing's search volume is lower than Google's, it often captures a unique audience, including users who may not be active on Google.
- **Lower Competition:** Due to its lower search volume compared to Google, Bing Ads often has lower competition and, consequently, lower cost-per-click (CPC) for certain keywords. This can be advantageous for advertisers with more limited budgets.
- **Demographic Targeting:** Bing Ads provides demographic targeting options, allowing advertisers to reach specific age groups, genders, and other demographic segments.
- **Native Advertising:** Bing Ads allows advertisers to create native ads that seamlessly blend with the appearance of the search results page, providing a non-disruptive advertising experience for users.
- **Import Campaigns from Google Ads:** To streamline campaign management, advertisers can easily import

campaigns from Google Ads into Bing Ads, making it more efficient to run campaigns on both platforms.

When exploring PPC platforms, a comprehensive strategy may involve utilising both Google Ads and Bing Ads to maximise your reach across different user demographics and search preferences. Each platform has its strengths, and the choice between them depends on factors such as target audience, budget, and advertising goals. By understanding the unique features and advantages of Google Ads and Bing Ads, advertisers can create a well-rounded PPC strategy that aligns with your business objectives.

Benefits of PPC: While I am a huge advocate for organic first, PPC can play a really valuable role in your wider and long-term marketing strategy. Let's discover the advantages of PPC advertising, such as instant visibility, targeting options, and measurable results and understand how it complements your SEO efforts.

PPC advertising offers several advantages that contribute to its effectiveness as a digital marketing strategy. One notable benefit is the instant visibility it provides to businesses. Unlike organic methods that may take time to gain traction, PPC allows advertisers to appear prominently on search engine results pages (SERPs) as soon as their campaigns are launched. This immediate visibility is crucial for time-sensitive promotions, product launches, or events. Additionally, PPC offers extensive targeting options, enabling advertisers to tailor their campaigns to specific demographics, locations, and even device types. This precision ensures that ads are delivered to the most relevant audience, increasing the likelihood of engagement and conversions.

Moreover, the measurable results inherent in PPC campaigns empower advertisers to track and analyse performance comprehensively. Key metrics such as clicks, impressions, conversion rates, and return on investment (ROI) can be monitored in real-time, allowing for data-driven decision-making and optimisation. This transparency ensures that businesses can continually refine their strategies for better outcomes.

Importantly, PPC and SEO (Search Engine Optimisation) are symbiotic strategies that, when used in conjunction, can amplify the overall impact of a digital marketing campaign. While SEO focuses on organic, unpaid methods to improve a website's visibility in search results over time, PPC delivers immediate visibility through paid advertising. By leveraging both approaches, businesses can achieve a holistic online presence, maximising their chances of reaching and engaging their target audience effectively. PPC and SEO can inform each other's strategies, with insights from PPC campaigns aiding in keyword research and content optimisation for SEO, ultimately leading to a more comprehensive and successful digital marketing strategy.

Setting Up Google Ads Campaigns

Account Setup: Setting up a Google Ads account involves several steps, including choosing the right campaign type, configuring payment settings, and defining your target audience. Here's a brief walkthrough of the process (correct at time of writing – Google may make changes over time):

1. **Visit Google Ads Website:**
   - Go to the Google Ads website (ads.google.com) and click on the "Start Now" button.

2. **Sign in or Create an Account:**
   - Sign in with your existing Google account or create a new one. If you're creating a new account, follow the prompts to enter the necessary information.

3. **Create Your First Campaign:**
   - After signing in, click on the "+ New Campaign" button to start creating your first campaign.

4. **Choose a Campaign Goal:**
   - Select a campaign goal based on your advertising objectives. Google Ads offers various campaign types, including:
     - **Search:** Show text ads on Google Search when people search for relevant keywords.
     - **Display:** Display visual ads across the Google Display Network.
     - **Shopping:** Promote your products with shopping ads.
     - **Video:** Advertise on YouTube and across the web with video ads.
     - **App:** Promote your app across different Google platforms.

5. **Select Campaign Type and Subtype:**
   - Based on your goal, choose the specific campaign type and subtype. For example, if you selected "Search," you may further specify whether it's for website traffic, leads, or sales.

6. **Configure Campaign Settings:**
   - Set up your campaign by providing details such as campaign name, location targeting, language preferences, bidding strategy, and daily budget. Customise these settings based on your specific marketing goals.

7. **Create Ad Groups:**
   - Organise your campaign by creating ad groups. Ad groups contain a set of related keywords and ads. For example, if you're running a Search campaign, each ad group might focus on a specific product or service.

8. **Create Ads:**
   - Craft compelling ads for each ad group. For text ads, write engaging headlines and descriptions. If you're running a Display, Shopping, Video, or App campaign, create visually appealing and relevant assets.

9. **Configure Payment Settings:**
   - Set up your payment method by providing billing information. Google Ads offers various payment options, including credit cards and bank accounts. Choose the one that suits your preferences.

10. **Define Target Audience:**
    - Specify your target audience based on demographics, interests, and behaviours. Use audience targeting options to narrow down your

reach and ensure your ads are shown to the most relevant users.

11. **Review and Launch:**
    - Review all your campaign settings, ad groups, and ads. Once you're satisfied, click on the "Launch" or "Submit" button to set your campaign live.

Remember to continuously monitor and optimise your campaigns based on performance metrics to maximise their effectiveness over time. Regularly analyse data, adjust bidding strategies, and refine ad content to achieve your desired outcomes.

Keyword Research for PPC: To achieve successful campaigns it is essential to understand the crucial role of keyword research in PPC campaigns. Learn how to choose the right keywords and structure your ad groups effectively.

Here are four of my top tips to achieve success in keyword research and ad group structuring:

Understand Your Audience and Business Goals:
    Start by gaining a deep understanding of your target audience and their search behaviours. Identify the keywords and phrases they are likely to use when searching for products or services related to your business. Align your keyword choices with the specific goals of your PPC campaign, whether it's driving website traffic, generating leads, or promoting sales.

Use Keyword Research Tools:
    Leverage keyword research tools such as Google Keyword Planner, SEMrush, Ubersuggest or Ahrefs to discover relevant keywords and assess their search volume, competition, and cost-per-click (CPC). These tools provide valuable insights into the popularity and competitiveness of

keywords, helping you make informed decisions about which ones to target.

Focus on Relevance and Match Types:
Prioritise relevance in your keyword selection. Choose keywords that closely match the products or services you offer. Utilise different match types (broad match, phrase match, exact match, and broad match modifier) strategically to control the specificity of your targeting. This ensures that your ads are shown to users searching with intent closely aligned with your offerings.

Create Well-Structured Ad Groups:
Organise your keywords into well-structured ad groups based on common themes or topics. Each ad group should have a specific focus, allowing you to tailor ad copy and landing pages to match the selected keywords. This enhances the relevance of your ads, improving the overall quality score and increasing the likelihood of achieving higher ad rankings.

Understanding the nuances of keyword research and ad group structuring empowers advertisers to fine-tune their PPC campaigns for maximum effectiveness. By aligning keywords with audience intent, utilising research tools, emphasising relevance, and creating organised ad groups, businesses can optimise their PPC efforts, reaching the right audience with compelling and targeted messaging. Regularly monitor and adjust your keyword strategy based on campaign performance to ensure ongoing success.

Budgeting and Bidding Strategies

Setting a Budget: Determine your PPC budget, considering factors like your business goals, competition, and the cost per click (CPC).

I suggest using some of these budget allocation techniques:

Goal-Based Budgeting: Align your PPC budget with your business goals. If the primary goal is to drive website traffic, allocate a budget that supports a higher click volume. For goals like lead generation or sales, allocate budgets to focus on conversion-driven campaigns.

Competitive Analysis: Assess the competitiveness of your industry and the chosen keywords. In highly competitive markets, you might need a larger budget to maintain visibility. Analyse competitor strategies and adjust your budget accordingly to stay competitive.

Cost Per Click (CPC) Consideration: Understand the average CPC for your selected keywords and industry. If your keywords have a higher CPC, you may need a larger budget to generate a significant volume of clicks. Factor in the potential cost of each click when setting your overall budget.

Seasonal Adjustments: Consider seasonal fluctuations in demand and adjust your budget accordingly. During peak seasons or promotional periods, you might allocate a higher budget to capitalise on increased search volume and consumer interest.

Daily Budget Management:

Flexible Daily Budgets: PPC platforms often allow you to set a daily budget for your campaigns. Monitor the performance regularly and adjust daily budgets based on the campaign's success. Allocate more budget to top-performing campaigns or ad groups to maximize results.

Bid Adjustments:
>Utilise bid adjustments to allocate more budget to high-converting audiences or specific demographics. Bid adjustments allow you to optimise your spend based on the performance of different segments, enhancing the efficiency of your budget allocation.

Ad Schedule Adjustments: Analyse the performance of your ads during different times of the day or days of the week. Adjust your ad schedule and daily budgets to allocate more budget to periods when your target audience is most active or when conversions are more likely to occur.

Performance Monitoring and Optimization: Regularly monitor key performance metrics such as click-through rate (CTR), conversion rate, and cost per conversion. Use this data to identify underperforming areas and reallocate budget to campaigns or ad groups that are driving better results.

Budget Pacing Tools:
>Some PPC platforms offer budget pacing tools that help evenly distribute your budget throughout the campaign period. This prevents exhausting your daily budget too quickly, ensuring a consistent and sustained presence in the ad auctions.

By combining a strategic approach to budget allocation with proactive daily budget management, businesses can optimise their PPC spending for maximum impact. Regularly assess and adjust your budgeting strategy based on the evolving needs of your business, industry competition, and campaign performance.

Bidding Strategies: PPC offers a range of bidding strategies that advertisers can choose based on their campaign goals, preferences, and level of control. Here's a brief overview of various bidding strategies:

Manual Bidding:
Description: Advertisers manually set bids for clicks, impressions, or conversions. This strategy provides maximum control but requires active management so is very time consuming.

Use Case: Ideal for experienced advertisers who want precise control over bid adjustments and budget allocation. It is a strategy that can work well if you have sufficient people working in your business to focus a majority of their time on this.

Automated Bidding:
Description: Ad platforms use machine learning to automatically set bids based on historical data and user behaviour patterns.

Use Case: Suitable for advertisers seeking a hands-off approach, especially when dealing with large datasets. Examples include Google's "Maximise Clicks" and "Enhanced Cost Per Click (ECPC)." This is a good strategy if you have limited people available to work on this or less marketing expertise.

Target CPA (Cost Per Acquisition):
Description: Advertisers set a target cost per acquisition, and the system adjusts bids to meet that goal while maximising conversions.

Use Case: Effective for advertisers focused on acquiring customers at a specific cost, particularly in conversion-driven campaigns.

Target ROAS (Return On Ad Spend):

Description: Advertisers set a target return on ad spend, and the system adjusts bids to maximise the return on investment.

Use Case: Suitable for e-commerce businesses looking to optimise for revenue generation and achieve a specific return on ad spend.

Maximize Conversions:

Description: The system automatically sets bids to get the most conversions within the specified budget.

Use Case: Ideal for advertisers focused on driving as many conversions as possible within their budget constraints.

Target Impression Share:

Description: Advertisers set a target percentage of impression share, and the system adjusts bids to achieve that share.

Use Case: Useful for advertisers aiming to maximise visibility or maintain a competitive presence in ad auctions.

Bid Modifiers (Device, Location, Time):

Description: Advertisers adjust bids based on specific criteria such as device type, geographic location, or time of day.

Use Case: Allows for fine-tuning bids based on the performance of different segments, optimising for specific user behaviours.

Enhanced CPC (ECPC):

Description: Advertisers enable the system to automatically adjust manual bids based on the likelihood of conversion.

Use Case: Combines manual control with automated bid adjustments, suitable for advertisers seeking a balance between control and efficiency.

Choosing the right bidding strategy depends on your campaign goals, budget, and the level of control you desire. Regularly monitor and adjust your bidding strategy based on campaign performance to achieve optimal results.

Monitoring and Optimising PPC Campaigns

It is important to keep monitoring your ad campaigns to ensure you are getting the results need for success, and if you need to adapt your campaigns to ensure they are fully optimised for cost-effectiveness and results. Not doing so can lead to mounting costs and wasted time and money.

Ad Copy and Landing Page Optimisation: Crafting compelling ad copy and ensuring a seamless transition to a relevant landing page are critical for the success of your PPC campaigns.

Ad Extensions and Ad Quality: Explore ad extensions to enhance the visibility of your ads and improve click-through rates. Google's Ad Quality Score is a tool that you can use to impact your campaigns.

A/B Testing and Performance Metrics: Discover how to run A/B tests on your ads and landing pages to identify what works best. Understand and monitor your key performance metrics like click-through rate (CTR), conversion rate, and Quality Score.

Ad Scheduling and Geo-Targeting: Learn how to schedule your ads to run during peak times and how to target specific geographic locations to maximise your reach.

Chapter Summary

Pay-Per-Click advertising is a dynamic and data-driven approach to digital marketing. By mastering the setup, budgeting, bidding, and optimisation of your PPC campaigns, you'll be able to drive targeted traffic to your website and achieve your marketing objectives.

In the coming chapters, we'll explore more digital marketing strategies, including email marketing, social media marketing, and content marketing, to create a comprehensive and integrated approach to promoting your small business online.

6. Email Marketing

Email marketing remains one of the most effective tools in a small business's digital marketing arsenal.

This chapter explores the nuances of email marketing, from building and managing an email list to crafting effective email campaigns and implementing automation and segmentation strategies.

Building and Managing an Email List

List Building Strategies: Discover effective methods for building your email list, including opt-in forms on your website, content incentives, social media promotions, and more.

Opt-in Forms on Your Website:
Process:
- Create compelling opt-in forms on key pages of your website.
- Strategically place forms in high-visibility areas, such as the homepage, blog, or landing pages.
- Use clear and persuasive copy to encourage visitors to subscribe.
- Integrate the forms with your email marketing platform for seamless data collection.

Tips:
- Offer an incentive (e.g., a discount, ebook, or exclusive content) to encourage sign-ups.
- A/B test different form designs and placements to optimise conversion rates.

Content Incentives:
Process:
- Create valuable content such as ebooks, whitepapers, or webinars.
- Promote these content incentives across your digital channels.
- Require email sign-up for access to the content.
- Automatically add new subscribers to your email list.

Tips:

- Ensure the content is genuinely valuable to your target audience.
- Promote content incentives through social media, blog posts, and email campaigns.

Social Media Promotions:
   Process:
- Leverage your social media platforms to promote email sign-ups.
- Run contests or giveaways with entry requirements being email subscription.
- Share sneak peeks of exclusive content available to subscribers.
- Include a clear call-to-action directing followers to your website's opt-in forms.

   Tips:
- Use visually appealing graphics and compelling copy in your social media posts.
- Regularly remind your social media audience of the benefits of subscribing.

List Segmentation: Understand the importance of segmenting your email list based on demographics, behaviours, or preferences. Segmenting allows you to send more personalised and relevant content.

Demographic Segmentation:
   Process:
- Collect data on subscriber demographics (age, location, gender, etc.).
- Use this data to segment your email list into distinct demographic groups.

- Tailor content and promotions to the specific interests of each segment.
- Implement personalised email campaigns for each demographic segment.

Tips:
- Gather demographic data through sign-up forms or surveys.
- Regularly update and refine segments as your subscriber base evolves.

Behavioural Segmentation:

Process:
- Track user behaviour such as email opens, clicks, and purchase history.
- Identify patterns and preferences in subscriber behaviour.
- Create segments based on engagement levels or specific actions.
- Send targeted emails based on these behavioural segments.

Tips:
- Implement marketing automation to track and respond to user behaviour in real-time.
- Use behavioural data to send personalised product recommendations or re-engagement campaigns.

Preference Segmentation:

Process:
- Allow subscribers to indicate their content preferences during sign-up.
- Segment your list based on these preferences (e.g., product interests, content topics).

- Send customised content that aligns with subscriber preferences.
- Implement preference centres for subscribers to update their interests.

Tips:

- Regularly review and update preference options to accommodate changing interests.
- Use preference data to create highly relevant and engaging content.

List Hygiene: I can't stress the value of this one enough! Apply list hygiene practices to maintain a clean and engaged email list.

Unsubscribe Handling:
Process:

- Include a clear and easy-to-find unsubscribe link in all marketing emails.
- Honour unsubscribe requests promptly to maintain compliance with regulations (in the UK that's the Data Protection Act 2018, which is the UK's implementation of the General Data Protection Regulation (GDPR).
- Regularly audit your unsubscribe process to ensure its effectiveness.
- Use preference centres to allow subscribers to manage their email preferences.

Tips:

- Keep the unsubscribe process simple and straightforward to avoid frustration.
- Monitor unsubscribe rates and analyse feedback to identify potential issues.

Bounce Management:

Process:

- Regularly clean your email list to remove invalid or non-existent email addresses.
- Monitor bounce rates after each email campaign.
- Identify and investigate hard bounces, which indicate permanent delivery failures.
- Consider using email verification tools to validate email addresses.

Tips:

- Implement double opt-in to verify the accuracy of new email addresses.
- Periodically re-engage inactive subscribers to prevent deliverability issues.

By implementing these list building, segmentation, and hygiene strategies, you can cultivate a more engaged and responsive email list, ensuring that your email marketing efforts are both effective and compliant with industry regulations. Regularly evaluate and adjust these strategies based on evolving subscriber behaviour and industry best practices.

Crafting Effective Email Campaigns

Email Content and Design: Creating engaging email content and visually appealing designs is paramount for successful email marketing campaigns. A well-crafted email not only captures the attention of your audience but also compels them to take the desired actions. To achieve this, start by understanding your audience and tailoring your content to their interests, needs, and preferences. Personalisation is key, as it fosters a sense of connection and relevance. Use segmentation data to deliver content that resonates with specific groups, whether based on demographics, behaviours, or preferences.

When it comes to design, simplicity and clarity are fundamental. A clean and visually appealing layout enhances readability and ensures that your message is easily understood. Incorporate eye-catching visuals, such as high-quality images or compelling graphics, to complement your content and reinforce your brand identity. Consistency in branding elements, including colours, fonts, and logos, helps establish a cohesive and recognizable email presence.

Moreover, in the digital age, mobile responsiveness is non-negotiable. A significant portion of email opens occurs on mobile devices, and if your emails are not optimised for various screen sizes, you risk losing a substantial portion of your audience. Responsive design ensures that your email adapts seamlessly to different devices, providing a user-friendly experience. Pay attention to concise subject lines and preheader text, as these elements often determine whether recipients will open your email on their mobile devices. By embracing these best practices in content creation, design, and mobile optimisation, you enhance the overall impact of your email campaigns and increase the likelihood of positive engagement and conversions.

Subject Lines and Personalization: Subject lines play a pivotal role in determining the success of an email campaign, as they are the first point of contact with recipients. The significance of subject lines lies in their ability to capture attention and entice recipients to open the email. A compelling subject line should be concise, intriguing, and relevant to the content inside. Including elements like urgency, curiosity, or a clear value proposition can increase the likelihood of recipients engaging with your email. A/B testing different subject lines allows you to analyse their effectiveness and refine your approach based on what resonates most with your audience.

Personalisation takes email marketing to a more individualised and impactful level. By incorporating personalisation elements in subject lines and throughout the email content, you create a tailored experience for each recipient. This can range from addressing recipients by their first name to customising content based on their previous interactions or preferences. Personalised emails have been shown to significantly improve open rates and engagement. Understanding your audience's preferences and behaviours enables you to segment your email list effectively and deliver targeted, personalised content that speaks directly to the needs and interests of each segment. Ultimately, recognising the significance of subject lines and embracing personalisation empowers you to create more compelling and relevant email campaigns that resonate with your audience and drive better performance metrics.

Call to Action (CTA): Crafting compelling calls to action (CTAs) is a critical aspect of email marketing, as it directly influences the actions you want recipients to take. The effectiveness of a CTA lies in its ability to be clear, specific, and persuasive. Clearly communicate the desired action you want the recipient to take, whether it's making a purchase, signing up for an event, or downloading content. Use action-oriented language that instils a sense of urgency or excitement, prompting immediate engagement.

In addition to clarity, relevance is key when designing CTAs. Ensure that the CTA aligns seamlessly with the content of the email and provides value to the recipient. Whether you're promoting a limited-time offer, inviting them to a personalised event, or enticing them with exclusive content, the CTA should be an extension of the overall message. Testing different variations of CTAs, including text, colour, and placement, through A/B testing helps identify what resonates most with your audience and maximizes conversion rates.

Moreover, the placement of CTAs within the email is crucial. Whether positioned prominently at the beginning, middle, or end of the email, the CTA should be strategically placed where it naturally fits into the flow of the content. Ensure that the CTA stands out visually, making it easy for recipients to locate and act upon. Crafting compelling CTAs involves a thoughtful blend of persuasive language, visual appeal, and strategic placement, ultimately motivating recipients to take the desired actions you've outlined in your email marketing campaign.

Automation and Segmentation for Small Businesses

Email Automation: Let's take a few moments to delve into the world of email automation, which allows you to send targeted messages based on user behaviour.

Email automation has revolutionised the way businesses communicate with their audience, allowing for personalised and timely interactions. Understanding key automated email campaigns like drip campaigns, welcome series, and abandoned cart emails can significantly enhance your email marketing strategy.

Drip Campaigns: Drip campaigns, also known as nurture campaigns, involve sending a series of pre-scheduled emails to a specific segment of your audience over a set period. These campaigns are designed to guide recipients through a predefined journey, delivering relevant content at each stage of the customer lifecycle. For instance, a drip campaign might start with a welcome email, followed by educational content, and eventually lead to promotional offers. Drip campaigns are powerful tools for nurturing leads, building relationships, and driving conversions, as they provide a consistent and automated communication flow.

Welcome Series: A welcome series is a specialised form of drip campaign triggered when a subscriber joins your email list. It typically consists of a sequence of emails aimed at introducing new subscribers to your brand, products, or services. The welcome series is an opportunity to make a positive first impression, share valuable information, and encourage specific actions. This might include setting expectations for future communications, promoting key products, or inviting subscribers to engage with your website or social media. A well-crafted welcome series establishes a strong foundation for ongoing engagement and customer loyalty.

Abandoned Cart Emails: Abandoned cart emails are targeted messages sent to individuals who have added items to their online shopping cart but have not completed the purchase. These automated emails aim to recover potentially lost sales by reminding customers of their abandoned items and encouraging them to finalise their transactions. Abandoned cart emails often include persuasive messaging, product images, and sometimes offer incentives such as discounts or free shipping to incentivise the completion of the purchase. This type of automation leverages behavioural data to deliver timely and relevant messages, addressing a common point of friction in the online shopping experience.

Incorporating these automated email campaigns into your strategy enables you to engage with your audience in a personalised and efficient manner. By leveraging automation for drip campaigns, welcome series, and abandoned cart emails, you can build stronger connections, drive conversions, and streamline your marketing efforts.

Segmentation Strategies: Implement advanced segmentation strategies to send more relevant content to your subscribers. Let's discuss dynamic content, behaviour-triggered emails, and nurturing sequences.

Dynamic Content: Dynamic content is a powerful feature in email marketing that enables marketers to personalise the content of an email based on the recipient's characteristics or preferences. This level of personalisation goes beyond simply addressing the recipient by name. Dynamic content allows you to customise images, text, offers, and even entire sections of an email based on data such as demographics, location, or past behaviour. For example, an e-commerce brand can showcase different product recommendations for each recipient, tailoring the content to individual preferences. This level of personalisation enhances relevance, engagement, and ultimately, the effectiveness of your email campaigns.

Behaviour-Triggered Emails: Behaviour-triggered emails are automated messages that are sent in response to specific actions or behaviours exhibited by a user. These triggers can include actions such as website visits, clicks on certain links, or interactions with previous emails. For instance, if a subscriber clicks on a particular product link in an email, a behaviour-triggered email can be set to follow up with additional information about that product or offer a special promotion. These emails are highly targeted, timely, and responsive to the user's demonstrated interests or actions, providing a personalised experience that fosters engagement and encourages further interaction.

Nurturing Sequences: Nurturing sequences, also known as lead nurturing or drip campaigns, are a series of automated emails designed to guide leads through the sales funnel. These sequences are crafted to deliver relevant and valuable content at different stages of the buyer's journey, helping to build trust and move prospects towards conversion. Nurturing sequences are not just about pushing sales messages; they are about providing educational content, addressing pain points, and progressively introducing more product-focused information. By delivering content aligned with the recipient's needs and behaviour, nurturing sequences establish a continuous and meaningful dialogue with leads, ultimately increasing the likelihood of conversion.

Incorporating dynamic content, behaviour-triggered emails, and nurturing sequences into your email marketing strategy elevates your ability to engage with your audience on a personal level. These tactics leverage automation to deliver timely, relevant, and tailored messages that resonate with recipients, driving higher levels of engagement and fostering stronger relationships over time.

A/B Testing and Analytics: One of the keys to success across your digital marketing efforts is understanding A/B testing. Let's look at running A/B tests on your email campaigns to improve open rates and conversion rates. Analyse email campaign performance metrics and adjust your strategy accordingly.

Running A/B tests on your email campaigns is a crucial practice to optimise performance, enhance engagement, and improve overall effectiveness. To initiate A/B testing, start by identifying a specific element you want to test. This could include variations in subject lines, email copy, calls to action, images, or even the timing of your campaigns. For example, if you're testing subject lines, create two versions (A and B) with slight differences, such as tone, length, or urgency. Ensure that the changes align with your campaign goals, whether it's increasing open rates or driving conversions.

Next, segment your audience randomly into two groups, with each group receiving one version of the email (A or B). It's essential to control variables to accurately measure the impact of the tested element. Monitor key metrics such as open rates, click-through rates, and conversion rates for each version. Analysing these metrics provides valuable insights into which variation performs better with your audience. After sufficient data is collected, declare a winner based on the predetermined success metric (e.g., higher open rates), and implement the winning version for future campaigns.

In addition to A/B testing, regularly analyse the broader performance metrics of your email campaigns. Metrics like overall open rates, click-through rates, conversion rates, and unsubscribe rates offer insights into the overall health and effectiveness of your email marketing strategy. Identify patterns and trends in these metrics to understand what resonates with your audience and what might need adjustment. For instance, if you notice a decline in open rates, consider testing different subject lines or revisiting your segmentation strategy. Continuous analysis and adaptation based on performance data allow you to refine your email strategy over time, ensuring it remains aligned with the evolving preferences and behaviours of your audience.

Chapter Summary

Email marketing can be a powerful channel for nurturing leads, engaging with customers, and driving conversions. By carefully building and managing your email list, crafting effective email campaigns, and implementing automation and segmentation, you can leverage this tool to create a more personalised and engaging experience for your audience, achieving significantly improved results for your business.

In the upcoming chapters, we'll continue to explore other digital marketing strategies, such as social media marketing, content marketing, and analytics, to build a comprehensive and integrated approach to promoting your small business online.

7. Social Media Marketing

Social media has become an integral part of our daily lives, making it a powerful platform for small businesses to connect with their audience. There are a number of key social media platforms and it is key to understand which ones are right for your business, trying to have a consistent presence on all of them is a bit like throwing enough mud at the walls just to see if some of it sticks – a lot of effort for limited results!

This chapter explores the world of social media marketing, focusing on creating a social media content calendar, paid advertising strategies, and measuring social media ROI.

Creating a Social Media Content Calendar

Content Planning and Strategy: A well-defined content strategy for social media is integral to the success of any business aiming to make a meaningful impact in the digital landscape. It serves as the blueprint for creating, publishing, and managing content that not only resonates with your target audience but also aligns seamlessly with your overarching business goals. The strategic planning involved in crafting a content strategy ensures that your social media efforts are purposeful, cohesive, and contribute meaningfully to your brand narrative.

One fundamental aspect of a robust content strategy is understanding how your content aligns with your business goals. Whether your primary objectives are brand awareness, lead generation, customer engagement, or driving sales, your content should be tailored to support and reinforce these goals. For instance, if your aim is to enhance brand awareness, your content strategy might focus on creating shareable and visually appealing content that introduces and reinforces your brand identity. On the other hand, if lead generation is a priority, your strategy may involve crafting content that encourages audience interaction, prompting them to share contact information or express interest in your products or services.

Equally crucial is ensuring that your content strategy resonates with your target audience. This involves a deep understanding of your audience's preferences, behaviours, and pain points. Tailoring your content to address the specific needs and interests of your audience fosters a stronger connection, increases engagement, and positions your brand as a valuable resource. By incorporating audience-centric elements into your content strategy, such as personalised messaging, relevant topics, and a consistent brand voice, you create a social media presence that not only attracts attention but also cultivates a loyal and responsive community.

In essence, a well-defined content strategy for social media is a strategic roadmap that guides your brand's online presence. It ensures that every piece of content serves a purpose, contributes to your business objectives, and resonates with the audience you aim to reach. By aligning content creation with business goals and audience preferences, you lay the foundation for a compelling and effective social media presence that goes beyond mere visibility, driving meaningful results for your business.

Content Types and Themes: Diversifying your content types is a key strategy in creating a vibrant and engaging social media presence. Understanding the strengths and nuances of various content formats allows you to cater to the diverse preferences of your audience. Posts, the fundamental building blocks of your social media strategy, come in various forms, from text-based updates to video and image-rich posts. These serve as the foundation of your content calendar, delivering regular and timely messages to your audience. Complementing these are stories, ephemeral content that offers a sense of immediacy and exclusivity. Stories are particularly effective for showcasing behind-the-scenes glimpses, promotions, and time-sensitive updates, fostering a real-time connection with your audience.

Venturing into the realm of videos opens up a dynamic avenue for engagement. Whether it's short-form videos for quick consumption or longer-form content for in-depth exploration, videos have the power to convey emotions, tell compelling stories, and showcase products or services. Live videos, in particular, provide an authentic and interactive experience, allowing real-time engagement with your audience. Additionally, the incorporation of visual elements such as infographics and carousel posts adds variety to your content mix, catering to different learning and consumption styles.

Developing content themes is a strategic approach to ensure coherence and resonance in your messaging. Themes provide a cohesive narrative that aligns with your brand identity and speaks directly to the interests of your audience. Consider themes that showcase your brand's values, highlight user-generated content, or celebrate industry trends. By consistently weaving these themes into your content, you create a narrative arc that captivates and retains audience attention. Ensure that your themes align with current trends and conversations in your industry, demonstrating your brand's relevance and responsiveness.

Understanding your audience's preferences and behaviours is fundamental to developing content that resonates. Conduct audience research to gain insights into the type of content they engage with most. Analyse data such as engagement rates, click-through rates, and social media analytics to identify patterns and preferences. Leverage this information to refine your content strategy, tailoring themes and formats based on what resonates most with your audience. By constantly experimenting with and refining your content mix, you position your brand as dynamic, adaptable, and in tune with the evolving preferences of your audience, fostering sustained engagement and loyalty.

Posting Schedule: Establishing a consistent posting schedule is a fundamental aspect of maintaining an active and engaging social media presence. Consistency not only helps you stay on top of your audience's minds but also contributes to the algorithmic visibility on various platforms. Begin by understanding the peak times for engagement on each platform. For instance, on Instagram, posting during lunchtime or in the early evening might align with users' browsing habits, while on Twitter, weekday mornings are often considered prime times. It's essential to delve into platform-specific analytics and insights to pinpoint the optimal posting times based on your unique audience demographics and behaviours.

Social media management tools play a pivotal role in executing a well-organised posting schedule. These tools offer a range of features, including scheduling posts in advance, monitoring engagement metrics, and managing multiple platforms from a centralised dashboard. By using scheduling features effectively, you can plan and queue up posts in advance, ensuring a consistent flow of content even during busy periods. Additionally, these tools often provide analytics that can help refine your posting strategy over time. By analysing data on when your audience is most active and responsive, you can fine-tune your schedule for optimal engagement.

Moreover, the effectiveness of your posting schedule is closely tied to the quality and relevance of your content. Strive for a balance between promotional content, educational material, and engagement-driven posts. Consistency doesn't mean sacrificing variety; instead, it emphasises delivering diverse and valuable content consistently. Engage in conversations with your audience, respond promptly to comments, and leverage user-generated content to create a sense of community. A well-rounded and consistently executed posting schedule, supported by social media management tools and guided by platform-specific insights, strengthens your brand's online presence, fosters audience loyalty, and maximises the impact of your social media efforts.

Paid Advertising on Social Platforms

Paid social media advertising is a dynamic and influential component of digital marketing strategies, providing businesses with targeted and measurable avenues to reach their audience. Delving into this world involves understanding the diverse advertising options offered by major platforms like Facebook, Instagram, X (formerly Twitter), LinkedIn and TikTok.

> **Facebook and Instagram Advertising:** Facebook, being one of the largest social media platforms, offers an extensive suite of advertising options. From sponsored posts and carousel ads to video ads and dynamic ads, businesses can tailor their approach to fit their campaign goals. Instagram, owned by Facebook, seamlessly integrates with its advertising platform, allowing businesses to tap into Instagram's visually-driven audience with engaging photo and video content. The precise targeting capabilities of Facebook and Instagram ads enable businesses to reach specific demographics, interests, and behaviours.

> **X (formerly) Twitter Advertising:** X offers several advertising formats, each designed to maximise engagement within the platform's fast-paced environment. Promoted tweets, promoted accounts, and promoted trends allow businesses to amplify their presence and target specific user segments. Twitter's ad targeting options include demographics, interests, and keywords, enabling businesses to align their ads with trending topics or relevant conversations.

> **LinkedIn Advertising:** LinkedIn, known for its professional network, provides a unique advertising environment catering to B2B marketing. Sponsored content, sponsored InMail, and display ads enable businesses to target professionals based on their industry, job title, and company size. With a focus on professional connections, LinkedIn

advertising is particularly effective for lead generation, recruitment, and building brand authority within specific industries.

TikTok Advertising: In the realm of paid social media advertising, TikTok has emerged as a dynamic platform that uniquely captures the attention of a younger and highly engaged audience. TikTok advertising encompasses various formats, including In-Feed Ads, Branded Hashtag Challenges, and Branded Effects. In-Feed Ads appear seamlessly in users' "For You" feed, ensuring organic integration with the platform's content. Branded Hashtag Challenges encourage user participation by inviting them to create content around a specific hashtag, fostering user-generated engagement. Branded Effects allow businesses to create custom filters and effects, enhancing brand visibility in user-generated content. With its rapidly growing user base and innovative ad formats, TikTok presents a compelling opportunity for businesses looking to connect with a youthful and trend-conscious audience through creative and immersive advertising experiences.

Understanding the nuances of each platform's advertising options is crucial for businesses aiming to maximise the impact of their paid social media campaigns. It involves strategic decision-making regarding ad formats, targeting parameters, and budget allocation. By aligning these choices with campaign objectives, businesses can craft compelling paid social media strategies that resonate with their target audience, drive engagement, and achieve measurable results. Paid social media advertising serves as a powerful tool to amplify your brand message, expand your reach, and drive specific actions from your audience.

Ad Campaign Setup: Setting up an effective social media ad campaign involves meticulous planning and strategic decision-making across various elements. The process typically begins with defining your campaign objectives—whether it's increasing brand awareness, driving website traffic, generating leads, or encouraging specific actions. Once the goals are clear, delve into the targeting options available on the chosen social media platform. This step involves specifying the demographics, interests, and behaviours of your target audience. The more precise your targeting, the more efficiently your ads will reach the audience most likely to engage with your content.

Choosing the right ad format is crucial in conveying your message effectively. Social media platforms offer diverse formats, including image and video ads, carousel ads, slideshows, and more. Tailor your ad format to align with your campaign goals and the preferences of your target audience, and remember to use A/B testing to ensure you get the best resutls. Eye-catching visuals, concise copy, and a compelling call-to-action are essential elements in creating engaging ad content. Additionally, consider utilising features unique to each platform, such as Instagram's Stories format or X's Promoted Trends, to optimise your campaign for specific user behaviours.

Budget allocation is a critical aspect of ad campaign setup. Define your budget based on your campaign goals, the competitiveness of your target audience, and the duration of your campaign. Social media platforms often provide options for setting daily or lifetime budgets, offering flexibility in managing your advertising spend. Establish bid strategies, whether it's a cost-per-click (CPC) model, cost-per-thousand-impressions (CPM), or other bidding options provided by the platform. Regularly monitor and adjust your budget allocation based on the performance data obtained during the campaign.

Beyond these fundamental steps, ensure that you have tracking mechanisms in place to measure the success of your ad campaign. Set up conversion tracking, utilise UTM parameters in your URLs, and leverage analytics tools provided by the social media platforms.

Analyse key performance indicators (KPIs) such as click-through rates, engagement rates, and conversion rates to evaluate the effectiveness of your ad campaign. Continuous monitoring and optimisation throughout the campaign duration allow you to make data-driven decisions, ensuring your ad campaign remains aligned with your objectives and resonates with your target audience.

Ad Creatives and Copy: Creating compelling ad creatives and copy is a cornerstone of successful social media advertising, and can be a sticking point for many small businesses. Start by understanding the visual and narrative preferences of your target audience. Develop eye-catching visuals that resonate with your brand identity and evoke the desired emotions. Whether it's high-quality images, engaging videos, or interactive elements, ensure that your ad creative stands out amidst the noise of social media feeds. Leverage storytelling techniques to craft a narrative that not only captures attention but also communicates the unique value proposition of your product or service. Strive for a balance between creativity and clarity, ensuring that your message is easily understood and prompts immediate action.

When it comes to ad copy, brevity and impact are key. Craft concise and compelling copy that conveys your message within the limited attention span of social media users. Start with a strong headline that grabs attention, followed by clear and persuasive body text that highlights the benefits of your offering. Incorporate a compelling call-to-action that guides users on the specific action you want them to take, whether it's making a purchase, signing up for a newsletter, or exploring your website. A/B testing different ad copy variations allows you to identify what resonates most with your audience and refine your approach based on real-time performance data.

Aligning your ad creatives and copy with the unique features of each social media platform is crucial. Tailor your visuals and messaging to suit the platform's audience demographics and user behaviour. Additionally, consider incorporating platform-specific features such as Instagram's carousel format, X and TikTok's trending hashtags, or LinkedIn's professional tone to enhance the relevance and effectiveness of your ads. By adhering to these best practices, you elevate your ad creatives and copy from mere visuals and text to powerful tools that drive engagement, convey your brand story, and ultimately lead to conversions.

Measuring Social Media ROI

Defining Key Performance Indicators (KPIs): Identify the key metrics that matter for your social media marketing efforts, including reach, engagement, click-through rate, and conversion rate.

Identifying key metrics is fundamental for evaluating the success and impact of your social media marketing efforts. One crucial metric is reach, which gauges the number of unique users who have encountered your content. It provides insights into the potential audience size your content has reached and is instrumental in assessing your brand's visibility on social media platforms. Combining reach with impressions— the total number of times your content is displayed—offers a comprehensive understanding of how far your messages are disseminated across the social media landscape. Aiming for consistent growth in reach indicates an expanding brand presence, while analysing trends in impressions can reveal patterns of content resonance over time.

Engagement metrics, encompassing likes, comments, shares, and overall interactions, offer a qualitative assessment of audience interaction with your content. High engagement rates signify that your content is resonating with your audience, fostering a sense of community and connection. Monitoring engagement helps identify content preferences, allowing you to tailor future posts for maximum impact. Click-through rate (CTR) measures the proportion of users who clicked on your content compared to the total number of users who viewed it. This metric is particularly crucial for assessing the effectiveness of call-to-action elements in your posts or ads. A higher CTR indicates that your content is compelling enough to prompt users to take the desired actions, whether it's visiting your website, exploring product pages, or engaging with additional content. Combining these metrics provides a holistic view of your social media marketing performance, guiding strategic adjustments for improved engagement and conversions over time.

Analytics and Tracking Tools: Tracking social media metrics and campaign performance is made efficient and insightful through the use of various tools and analytics platforms. Social media analytics platforms such as Hootsuite, Sprout Social, and Buffer provide businesses with comprehensive dashboards to monitor and analyse key performance indicators (KPIs). These tools offer real-time insights into metrics such as engagement rates, reach, follower growth, and click-through rates. By aggregating data from different social media channels, these platforms allow businesses to have a centralised view of their social media performance, streamlining the monitoring process.

One of the primary functions of social media analytics tools is to assist businesses in interpreting data effectively. These platforms break down metrics into actionable insights, helping marketers understand which content performs best, when their audience is most active, and how their social media efforts contribute to overarching business goals. For instance, these tools may highlight peak engagement times, enabling businesses to schedule posts strategically. They can also provide demographic information about the audience, allowing for more targeted and personalised content creation. Analysing these insights empowers businesses to refine their social media strategies, optimise content for better engagement, and adapt their approach to align with the preferences and behaviours of their audience.

Interpreting social media data involves not only understanding individual metrics but also recognising patterns and trends over time. Businesses can identify successful campaigns, content themes that resonate most with their audience, and areas for improvement. For instance, a sudden spike in engagement might coincide with a specific type of content or campaign, signalling its success. Conversely, a drop in engagement could prompt a reassessment of content strategy or posting frequency. These analytics platforms often provide customisable reports, allowing businesses to tailor their data analysis based on their specific objectives. Regularly reviewing and interpreting social media metrics is an iterative process that enables businesses to refine their strategies, optimize their performance, and ultimately achieve meaningful results in the dynamic landscape of social media marketing.

Adjusting Strategies Based on Data: Making data-driven decisions based on a thorough analysis of social media metrics is essential for optimising your content strategy and advertising campaigns, ultimately leading to improved return on investment (ROI). Begin by regularly reviewing key performance indicators (KPIs) such as engagement rates, reach, click-through rates, and conversion rates. Identify patterns and trends within the data to understand what is resonating with your audience and what may need adjustment. For instance, if certain types of content consistently receive higher engagement, consider incorporating more of that content into your strategy.

Next, delve into the demographics and behaviours of your audience. Social media analytics platforms and tools, such as those described above, provide valuable insights into the age, gender, location, and interests of your audience. Use this information to tailor your content to better align with the preferences of your target demographic. If a particular segment of your audience engages more with specific content themes, adjust your content strategy to focus on those themes. This personalised approach enhances relevance, fostering stronger connections and increasing the likelihood of achieving the desired outcomes for your small business.

When it comes to advertising campaigns, closely analyse the performance of your paid efforts. Assess the effectiveness of different ad formats, targeting options, and messaging. If certain ads consistently outperform others, reallocate budget towards those high-performing ads to maximise impact. Additionally, leverage A/B testing to experiment with variations in ad creatives, copy, and targeting parameters. This iterative testing process allows you to refine your advertising strategy based on concrete performance data, ensuring that your campaigns evolve in alignment with audience preferences and market dynamics.

Adjusting your content strategy and advertising campaigns based on data-driven insights is an ongoing process. Regularly monitor social media metrics, compare performance against benchmarks, and adapt your approach accordingly. Implement changes incrementally to measure their impact on key metrics. By consistently refining your strategies in response to data, you can enhance the efficiency of your social media efforts, maximise engagement, and ultimately improve the return on investment for your content and advertising initiatives. This iterative and data-centric approach positions your brand to thrive in the ever-evolving landscape of social media marketing.

Chapter Summary

Social media marketing presents a unique opportunity to connect with your audience on a personal level, foster brand loyalty, and drive conversions. By creating a content calendar, exploring paid advertising options, and using tools to measure your social media ROI, you'll be well-equipped to leverage the power of social platforms for your small business.

In the remaining chapters, we'll continue to explore more digital marketing strategies, including content marketing, analytics, and online advertising, to build a comprehensive and integrated approach to promoting your small business online.

8. Content Marketing

Content marketing is a foundational element of your digital marketing strategy, allowing you to engage your audience, build trust, and establish your authority in your niche. It links into your social media marketing strategy and your paid marketing strategies.

This chapter explores the core aspects of content marketing, from developing a content strategy to distribution and performance tracking.

Developing a Content Strategy

Understanding Content Marketing: Content marketing is a strategic approach that revolves around creating and distributing valuable, relevant, and consistent content to attract and engage a target audience.

In the digital age, where consumers are inundated with information, content marketing stands out as a way to provide genuine value rather than intrusive advertising. It encompasses various forms of content, including blog posts, articles, videos, infographics, and more, tailored to meet the needs and interests of the audience.

The importance of content marketing lies in its ability to build trust, establish authority, and foster long-term relationships with audiences. By providing valuable information and solving their problems, you position your brand as a valuable resource, driving customer loyalty and engagement. Content marketing also complements other marketing strategies by creating a cohesive narrative that reinforces your brand message across various channels.

Identifying Your Target Audience: Let's revisit the importance of understanding your target audience and how it informs your content strategy.

Understanding your target audience is foundational for effective content marketing. This involves going beyond demographic data and delving into the psychographics, behaviours, and pain points of your audience. By creating detailed buyer personas, which are semi-fictional representations of your ideal customers, you gain a deeper understanding of their preferences, challenges, and aspirations.

This information informs your content strategy, allowing you to create content that resonates specifically with your target audience.

Knowing your audience's interests and communication preferences enables you to tailor your messaging and choose the most suitable content formats. This targeted approach enhances the relevance of your content, increasing the likelihood of capturing the attention and engagement of your intended audience. Identifying your target audience is an ongoing process, evolving as your business grows and as market dynamics change.

Setting Clear Objectives: Define your content marketing objectives, whether it's to increase brand awareness, drive website traffic, generate leads, or boost sales.

Setting clear objectives is essential for the success of your content marketing efforts. Begin by defining what you aim to achieve through your content. Whether it's increasing brand awareness, driving website traffic, generating leads, or boosting sales, having well-defined objectives provides a roadmap for your content strategy.

Each objective will require a tailored approach in terms of content creation, distribution, and measurement. For example, if your goal is brand awareness, your content may focus on storytelling and building a strong brand narrative. If lead generation is the priority, your content may include informative guides, webinars, or downloadable resources.

Setting clear objectives not only guides your content creation process but also allows you to measure the success of your efforts. Regularly assessing performance against these objectives enables you to adapt and refine your content strategy for continuous improvement.

Content Distribution and Promotion

In the realm of content marketing, a nuanced understanding of content types, effective promotion strategies, and meticulous planning through content calendars are indispensable. In this section we are going to delve into the diverse array of content types and formats available to marketers, elucidating how each serves distinct purposes. We will also explore the strategic promotion of content across various channels, emphasising the significance of a well-structured content distribution plan. Finally, we'll discuss the importance of a content calendar and its role in fostering consistency and audience engagement.

Content Types and Formats: Content marketing encompasses an extensive array of types and formats tailored to capture the attention of diverse audiences. Blog posts, with their informational and conversational style, are effective for engaging readers. Infographics distil complex information into visually appealing graphics, catering to those with visual learning preferences and just generally being quite simple for a user to digest. Videos provide a dynamic medium for storytelling and demonstrations, while eBooks offer in-depth explorations suitable for a more invested audience. Webinars combine audio and visual elements for interactive learning experiences. The key lies in discerning which format aligns best with your target audience and the goals of your content strategy. Understanding these diverse options allows for a strategic and varied approach, ensuring your content resonates with a broad spectrum of consumers.

Content Promotion Strategies: In small business digital marketing, you need to understand how to promote your content effectively through various channels, including social media, email marketing, and influencer outreach.

Creating exceptional content is only part of the equation; effective promotion is equally crucial. There are various content promotion strategies that a small business can utilise, emphasising the importance of a well-thought-out content distribution plan.

Social media platforms serve as powerful channels for content promotion, allowing for targeted outreach and engagement. Email marketing enables direct communication with your audience, while influencer outreach can amplify your content's reach.

Understanding how each strategy contributes to your overarching goals is vital. A comprehensive approach to content promotion ensures your carefully crafted material reaches the right audience at the right time, maximizing its impact and fostering a robust online presence.

Content Calendar and Scheduling: Create a content calendar to plan and organise your content publishing schedule. Consistency in content publishing can improve audience engagement significantly.

Consistency is a cornerstone of successful content marketing, and a well-organised content calendar plays a pivotal role in achieving it. This section guides you through the process of creating a content calendar, helping you plan and schedule your content publishing with precision. A content calendar not only ensures a steady flow of content but also allows for strategic alignment with key events, holidays, or product launches.

Consistent and timely content publication enhances audience engagement, as followers come to anticipate and rely on your regular updates. By adopting a structured approach to scheduling, you not only streamline your content production process but also cultivate a dedicated audience eager to consume your content regularly.

Tracking Content Performance

Measuring the effectiveness of your content marketing efforts is imperative for ongoing success. We have explored some of these aspects in previous chapters, but let's put them into context for your content strategy.

Key Performance Indicators (KPIs): Define the KPIs that matter for your content marketing strategy. Explore metrics like page views, time on page, social shares, and lead generation.

Defining and tracking Key Performance Indicators (KPIs) is fundamental for assessing the performance and impact of your content marketing strategy. Metrics such as page views reveal the extent of your content's reach, while time on page indicates audience engagement.

Social shares showcase the virality and resonance of your content within online communities. For businesses focused on lead generation, tracking conversion rates and the number of leads generated from specific pieces of content is paramount.

By aligning KPIs with your overall business goals, you gain actionable insights into what works well and where adjustments are needed in your content strategy, guiding continuous improvement.

Content Analytics Tools: As a small business you could use analytics tools to measure and track your content's performance data to make data-driven decisions. Understanding the tools available for content analytics is crucial for gaining a comprehensive view of your content's performance.

Analytics platforms such as Google Analytics, SEMrush, and HubSpot offer robust insights into various aspects of content performance. Whether it's understanding audience demographics, identifying traffic sources, or evaluating the effectiveness of specific keywords, content analytics tools empower you to make informed, data-driven decisions. Regularly monitoring these analytics ensures that your content strategy remains aligned with evolving audience preferences and industry trends.

Content Optimisation: Content optimisation is an iterative process based on the insights derived from performance data. This involves refining and enhancing your content to maximise its impact and relevance.

Analysing which pieces of content perform exceptionally well and understanding why provides valuable insights for optimisation. It may involve updating outdated content, repurposing successful pieces for different formats or channels, and fine-tuning your content strategy based on what resonates most with your audience.

The goal is to continually elevate the quality and effectiveness of your content, ensuring that it remains dynamic and responsive to the evolving needs and preferences of your target audience. Content optimisation is a continuous journey, aligning your strategy with data-driven insights for sustained success in the dynamic landscape of digital marketing.

Chapter Summary

Content marketing is a versatile and valuable approach to digital marketing. By developing a content strategy that aligns with your business goals, effectively distributing and promoting your content, and tracking performance through key metrics, you can create a content marketing strategy that resonates with your audience and delivers tangible results.

In the upcoming chapters, we'll continue to explore more digital marketing strategies, such as analytics, online advertising, and building customer loyalty, to create a comprehensive and integrated approach to promoting your small business online.

9. Analytics and Data-driven Decision Making

In the world of digital marketing, data is your most valuable asset. With data you can plan marketing effectively, review campaigns and develop a successful strategy.

In this chapter we're going to delve into the critical role of analytics and data-driven decision making in optimising your marketing efforts and achieving your business objectives.

Setting Up Google Analytics

What is Google Analytics? In the vast landscape of digital marketing, understanding and harnessing the power of data is paramount for success. Google Analytics stands out as a cornerstone tool, offering unparalleled insights into the performance of your website. From tracking visitor behaviour to measuring campaign effectiveness, Google Analytics provides a comprehensive view of how users interact with your online presence. Google Analytics is a powerful data tracking and analysis tool, guiding businesses and marketers through the process of setting up their Google Analytics account to unlock a wealth of actionable insights.

Significance of Google Analytics: Google Analytics serves as a digital compass, guiding businesses through the intricate terrain of online user behaviour. It empowers website owners to answer critical questions: Who is visiting my site? How do they navigate through its pages? What content resonates the most? Where do they drop off in the conversion funnel? By unravelling these mysteries, Google Analytics enables data-driven decision-making, helping your businesses optimise your online strategies.

Data Tracking Capabilities: Google Analytics tracks a myriad of data points, providing a holistic view of your website's performance. From the number of visitors and their geographical locations to the devices and browsers they use, the platform captures granular details. It goes beyond quantitative metrics, delving into user behaviour metrics like session duration, pages per session, and bounce rates. Understanding these metrics is akin to having a magnifying glass on your audience's digital journey, allowing you to pinpoint areas of improvement and capitalise on strengths. Additionally, Google Analytics plays a pivotal role in tracking the success of marketing campaigns, attributing conversions to specific channels and campaigns, enabling marketers to allocate resources effectively.

Setting Up a Google Analytics Account: The first step in unleashing the power of Google Analytics is setting up an account. Let's guide you through the process, emphasising the importance of accuracy in configuration. You start by creating a Google Analytics account using your Google credentials. Once the account is established, a new property is added for the website to be tracked. This involves entering essential details such as the website's name, URL, and industry category. Subsequently, a unique tracking code, known as the Google Analytics Tracking ID, is generated. This code is then embedded into the website's HTML, initiating the seamless flow of data from the website to the Google Analytics dashboard.

Configuring Views and Goals: After the initial setup, you proceed to configure views and goals within Google Analytics.

Views allow you to filter and segment data, providing a more tailored analysis based on specific parameters. For instance, setting up a view for a particular segment of the audience or a specific section of the website enables targeted insights. Goals, on the other hand, define key actions that are valuable to your business, such as completing a purchase or submitting a contact form.

Configuring goals allows Google Analytics to track and report on these critical interactions, providing a clear understanding of your website's conversion performance.

Navigating the Google Analytics Dashboard: Upon completion of the setup, you will be introduced to the

Google Analytics dashboard, a robust interface where the magic of data analysis unfolds.

The dashboard presents a comprehensive overview of key metrics, including real-time data, audience demographics, user behaviour, and acquisition channels. You can explore different reports, each offering a unique perspective on website performance.

Whether delving into the sources of website traffic, assessing the effectiveness of marketing campaigns, or understanding user engagement on specific pages, the dashboard serves as a command centre for informed decision-making.

Utilising Advanced Features: Beyond the basics, Google Analytics boasts a suite of advanced features that can elevate the depth and precision of data analysis. You can explore custom reports, delve into attribution models to understand the impact of various touchpoints on conversions, and leverage event tracking to capture specific user interactions.

Enhanced E-commerce tracking provides detailed insights for online retailers, tracking not only sales but also product performance and user behaviour throughout the purchase journey. Mastery of these advanced features empowers you to tailor Google Analytics to the unique needs and intricacies of your business.

Continuous Learning and Optimisation: The journey with Google Analytics is not a one-time setup; it's a continuous process of learning, optimisation, and adaptation.

Regularly reviewing reports, analysing trends, and interpreting data enables your business to stay agile in response to evolving user behaviours and market dynamics.

The platform's learning resources, including the Google Analytics Academy (a suite of free online courses), offer a wealth of tutorials and courses to deepen your understanding of the tool.

By consistently refining strategies based on the insights gained from Google Analytics, you can forge a path of sustained business growth and relevance in the digital landscape.

Defining Goals and Conversions: After the initial setup, it's important to configure views and goals within Google Analytics. Views allow you to filter and segment data, providing tailored insights based on specific parameters. For instance, you can set up a view for a particular audience segment or a specific section of your website. Goals, on the other hand, define critical actions that are valuable to your business, such as completing a purchase or submitting a contact form. Configuring goals enables Google Analytics to track and report on these pivotal interactions, offering a clear picture of your website's conversion performance.

Event Tracking: Setting up event tracking in Google Analytics allows you to capture and analyse specific user interactions on your website, such as clicks on buttons or form submissions. Here's a brief step-by-step guide:

1. **Access Google Analytics:**
   - Log in to your Google Analytics account.
   - Select the property and view where you want to set up event tracking.

2. **Navigate to the Admin Section:**

104

- In the lower-left corner, click on the "Admin" gear icon.

3. **Choose the Property:**
   - Under the "Property" column, select the property for which you want to set up event tracking.

4. **Configure Events:**
   - In the "Property" column, find and click on "Events" under the "Tracking Info" section.

5. **Create a New Event Category:**
   - Click on the "+ New Event Category" button.
   - Enter a name for your event category (e.g., "Button Clicks" or "Form Submissions").

6. **Define Event Actions:**
   - Under your newly created event category, click on "+ New Event Action."
   - Enter a descriptive name for your event action (e.g., "Clicked Button" or "Submitted Form").

7. **Set Up Event Labels (Optional):**
   - You can add labels to provide additional details about the event (e.g., the specific button or form).
   - Click on "+ New Event Label" and enter the label details.

8. **Configure Event Value (Optional):**
   - Assign a numeric value to the event if it represents a quantifiable action (e.g., a monetary value for a form submission).
   - Click on "+ New Event Value" and enter the value.

9. **Save Your Configuration:**
    - Click on the "Save" button to save your event configuration.

10. **Implement the Tracking Code:**
    - Once your event is configured, you'll receive a tracking code snippet.
    - Integrate this code into the relevant elements on your website, such as buttons or forms, to start tracking user interactions.

11. **Verify Event Tracking:**
    - After implementing the tracking code, use Google Analytics' Realtime reports or check the "Events" section under "Reports" to verify that your events are being tracked.

Interpreting Key Metrics

Understanding the key metrics in Google Analytics is essential for gaining insights into how users interact with your website. This section focuses on interpreting critical metrics related to traffic sources, user engagement, and conversion rate optimisation (CRO) to help you really make the best of use this amazing tool.

Traffic Sources and Channels: Begin by exploring where your website traffic originates. Google Analytics categorises traffic into various sources and channels, including organic search, social media, direct traffic, and referrals. Analysing the performance of each source provides valuable insights into the effectiveness of your marketing efforts.

For instance, you can identify which channels are driving the most traffic and understand user behaviour specific to each source. This knowledge enables you to refine your marketing strategy, allocating resources where they yield the best results. By delving into the intricacies of traffic sources, you gain a comprehensive understanding of your audience's online journey and optimise your online presence accordingly.

User Engagement Metrics: User engagement metrics offer a window into how visitors interact with your content. Key metrics such as bounce rate, time on page, and pageviews per session provide nuanced insights into user behaviour.

Bounce rate indicates the percentage of visitors who navigate away from the site after viewing only one page—an important metric for assessing the relevance of your landing pages. Time on page offers an understanding of how engaging your content is, while pageviews per session reveal the depth of user exploration.

By analysing these metrics, you can identify high-performing content and areas that may need improvement. This user-centric approach allows you to tailor your content strategy to meet the preferences and expectations of your audience, ultimately enhancing overall engagement.

Conversion Rate Optimisation (CRO): Conversion Rate Optimisation (CRO) is a crucial aspect of maximising the value of your website traffic. This involves optimizing your site and landing pages to improve the conversion rate, which is the percentage of visitors who take a desired action, such as making a purchase or submitting a form. Learn how to systematically enhance your website's performance through CRO strategies.

This includes A/B testing (which we have discussed before), where different versions of a webpage are compared to determine which performs better. By testing elements such as headlines, call-to-action buttons, or form placements, you can identify the most effective configurations that drive higher conversion rates. CRO is an iterative process that involves continuous testing, analysis, and refinement to create an optimised user experience that aligns with your business objectives.

Interpreting key metrics in Google Analytics provides a holistic view of your website's performance. By understanding traffic sources and channels, user engagement metrics, and the principles of Conversion Rate Optimisation, you can make informed decisions to enhance the effectiveness of your online presence and achieve your business goals.

Making Informed Marketing Decisions

In the dynamic landscape of digital marketing, making informed decisions is paramount for success.

Data-driven Strategy: Embrace a data-driven approach to marketing by continuously analysing and interpreting your data. Utilise tools like Google Analytics to gain deep insights into user behaviour, traffic sources, and campaign performance. Understand the importance of hypothesis testing and experimentation such as A/B testing, in refining your strategy. By formulating hypotheses and testing them against your data, you can uncover valuable insights that drive strategic decision-making.

Whether it's refining your target audience, optimising website content, or enhancing the effectiveness of your campaigns, a data-driven strategy empowers you to make decisions grounded in tangible evidence.

Adjusting Campaigns: Data analysis provides the foundation for identifying areas of improvement. Explore how data can inform changes to ad copy, audience targeting, and bidding strategies. For instance, if specific keywords are consistently underperforming, you can reallocate budget to more successful keywords. If a particular demographic responds well to your ads, adjust your targeting to focus on that segment.

The agility to adapt campaigns based on real-time data ensures that your marketing efforts remain aligned with evolving consumer behaviour and industry trends. This iterative process of analysis and adjustment is fundamental for optimising campaign performance and maximising your return on investment.

Performance Reporting: Create effective performance reports based on key metrics and Key Performance Indicators (KPIs).

Understanding how to compile and present data is essential for communicating the impact of your marketing efforts. Identify the most relevant metrics for your specific goals, whether it's conversion rates, click-through rates, or revenue generated. Craft clear and concise performance reports that highlight successes, challenges, and actionable insights.

Whether presenting to stakeholders, clients, or your team, effective reporting fosters a shared understanding of the data and facilitates informed decision-making. Learn how to visually represent data using charts and graphs to make complex information more digestible.

The ability to communicate the story behind the data is as crucial as the data itself in driving strategic decisions and fostering a culture of continuous improvement.

Making informed marketing decisions requires a commitment to a data-driven strategy, a willingness to adjust campaigns based on insights, and the ability to create compelling performance reports. By embracing data as a guiding force, you can can navigate the complexities of the digital landscape, refine your tactics, and achieve sustainable success in a dynamic and competitive environment.

Chapter Summary

Analytics and data-driven decision making are at the heart of successful digital marketing. By setting up Google Analytics, interpreting key metrics, and making informed marketing decisions based on data, you'll be able to continually refine your strategies and optimise your efforts for maximum impact.

In the last remaining chapters, we'll continue to explore more digital marketing strategies, including online advertising, customer loyalty, and future trends in small business digital marketing, to build a comprehensive and integrated approach to promoting your small business online.

10. Online Advertising and Budgeting

Online advertising is a powerful way to amplify your small business's reach and visibility in the digital landscape.

This chapter explores the world of online advertising, from budget allocation to ROI analysis and scaling your digital marketing efforts.

Budget Allocation for Digital Marketing

In the realm of digital marketing, effective budget allocation is a cornerstone of success.

In this section we'll delve into understanding digital advertising options, setting a digital marketing budget, and exploring strategies for optimal budget allocation across diverse channels.

Understanding Digital Advertising: To navigate the digital advertising landscape, one must first grasp the array of options available. Gain insights into the diverse range of digital advertising avenues, each with its unique strengths. Explore pay-per-click (PPC) advertising, where advertisers pay a fee each time their ad is clicked, making it a cost-effective way to drive targeted traffic for detailed explanation of this see Chapter 5). You might find it is right for your business to delve into display advertising, leveraging visual elements for brand exposure across websites.

Understand the power of social media advertising, tapping into the vast user bases of platforms like Facebook, Instagram, and X. Additionally, explore affiliate marketing, a performance-based strategy where businesses reward affiliates for driving customers to their site. A nuanced understanding of these options lays the foundation for strategic budget allocation.

Setting a Digital Marketing Budget: Determining your digital marketing budget is a critical step that involves aligning financial resources with business goals. Consider various factors, including your overarching business objectives, the characteristics of your target audience, and the competitive landscape in your industry.

Assess the specific goals of your digital marketing campaigns— whether it's driving website traffic, generating leads, or boosting sales. A well-defined budget sets the parameters for your marketing initiatives and ensures that financial resources are allocated in a way that maximises their impact.

Budget Allocation Strategies: With a clear budget in place, the next step is to explore strategies for allocating these resources across different digital marketing channels. Recognise that not all channels will yield the same return on investment (ROI) for every business.

Tailor your allocation based on the nature of your products or services and the preferences of your target audience. For instance, if your audience is highly engaged on social media, allocating a significant portion of your budget to social media advertising may be advantageous. Conversely, if your business thrives on search engine visibility, investing in PPC advertising could be a priority. Striking the right balance and adapting your budget allocation strategy based on performance metrics is essential for achieving a favourable ROI.

Effective budget allocation for digital marketing involves understanding the diverse landscape of digital advertising, setting a budget aligned with business goals, and employing strategic allocation strategies. As your business navigates the digital space, the ability to optimise budget allocation based on data-driven insights and the evolving needs of the target audience becomes a key driver of success.

ROI Analysis and Adjustments

Understanding the return on investment (ROI) for your digital marketing efforts is crucial for making informed decisions and optimising campaign performance.

Measuring ROI: Measuring ROI is foundational for assessing the success of your digital marketing campaigns. Learn how to quantify the return generated from your investment by identifying key performance indicators (KPIs).

Whether it's tracking website traffic, conversion rates, or revenue generated, align your KPIs with your campaign goals, effectively measuring ROI involves considering both the cost of your marketing efforts and the outcomes achieved. Understand the financial impact of your campaigns to make informed decisions on budget allocation and strategy refinement. A comprehensive grasp of ROI ensures that every pound spent on marketing is invested strategically, contributing to overall business growth.

Data Analysis for Optimisation: Once your campaigns are live, the real work begins with diving into the data collected. Explore how to conduct a thorough data analysis to glean actionable insights. Focus on critical metrics such as ad performance, conversion rates, and cost per acquisition (CPA).

Identify patterns, trends, and areas for improvement. For instance, if certain ads are consistently underperforming, analyse the elements contributing to this and make data-driven adjustments. Similarly, scrutinise the customer journey and pinpoint areas where conversions may be dropping off.

Through effective data analysis, you can optimise your campaigns in real-time, ensuring that your marketing efforts align with changing market dynamics and user behaviour.

A/B Testing and Optimisation: As we have already discussed more than once, implementing A/B testing is a powerful strategy for refining your advertising approaches. Explore how to set up controlled experiments to test different variables, such as ad creatives, targeting options, and bidding strategies.

By comparing the performance of two or more variations, you can identify which elements resonate most effectively with your audience. A/B testing provides actionable insights into what works and what doesn't, enabling you to make informed optimisations.

Whether it's refining ad copy to improve click-through rates or adjusting targeting parameters for better audience reach, A/B testing is a continuous process that fine-tunes your campaigns for maximum impact. Embracing a culture of optimisation through A/B testing ensures that your digital marketing strategies remain adaptive and responsive to the evolving dynamics of the online landscape.

ROI analysis and adjustments are integral components of a successful digital marketing strategy. By mastering the measurement of ROI, conducting insightful data analysis, and implementing A/B testing for continuous optimisation, enables your business to can refine your approaches and achieve sustained success.

Scaling Your Digital Marketing Efforts

Identifying Scalable Tactics: Discovering scalable tactics is pivotal for expanding and sustaining the impact of your digital marketing efforts.

One effective strategy is targeting new demographics. By identifying and reaching out to untapped audience segments, you broaden your reach and potential customer base. Conduct thorough market research to understand the characteristics, preferences, and behaviours of these new demographics.

Additionally, exploring new advertising platforms can provide fresh opportunities. The digital landscape is dynamic, and emerging platforms may offer innovative ways to connect with your audience.

Whether it's leveraging the visual appeal of Instagram or the professional network on LinkedIn, diversifying your advertising channels enhances your overall presence. Moreover, increasing your budget strategically can fuel growth. In 2024 TikTok is a platform that the vast majority of businesses can benefit from.

Analyse the performance of your existing campaigns and, if they demonstrate positive ROI, consider allocating additional budget to scale those efforts. Scaling doesn't always mean a drastic increase; it could involve incremental adjustments based on performance metrics.

Staying Competitive: In the fast-paced digital marketing arena, staying competitive requires a commitment to continual evolution and adaptation. To remain ahead of the competition, stay attuned to industry trends.

Regularly assess the digital marketing landscape for emerging technologies, shifts in consumer behaviour, and changes in search engine algorithms. Attend industry conferences, participate in webinars, and engage with relevant publications to stay informed. Adapt your strategies accordingly, incorporating innovative techniques and technologies to maintain relevance.

A proactive approach to staying competitive involves fostering a culture of learning within your team, encouraging professional development, and embracing a mindset of perpetual improvement. Furthermore, conduct regular competitor analysis.

Evaluate the strategies and tactics employed by your competitors, identifying both strengths and weaknesses. By understanding the competitive landscape, you can capitalise on opportunities and differentiate your brand effectively.

Monitoring and Reporting: Implementing robust monitoring and reporting systems is crucial as you scale your digital marketing efforts. These systems help you keep a finger on the pulse of your campaigns, ensuring that you can make informed adjustments in real-time.

Utilise analytics tools, such as Google Analytics, to track key performance indicators (KPIs). Regularly review metrics such as click-through rates, conversion rates, and return on investment. Set up automated reports to receive timely updates on campaign performance.

Adjust your strategies based on changing data. For instance, if a particular advertising platform is consistently delivering strong results, consider allocating more budget to capitalise on its success. Conversely, if certain channels or tactics are underperforming, be prepared to pivot and reallocate resources.

Transparent reporting is not only crucial for internal decision-making but also facilitates communication with stakeholders, clients, or team members. Presenting clear and concise reports ensures that everyone involved understands the impact of your efforts and supports data-driven decision-making.

As you scale, the ability to monitor and adapt will be instrumental in maintaining the efficiency and effectiveness of your digital marketing initiatives.

Chapter Summary

Online advertising can provide a substantial boost to your small business's digital marketing efforts. By allocating your budget wisely, analysing ROI, and scaling your campaigns, you can leverage online advertising to reach a wider audience, drive more conversions, and ultimately achieve your business goals.

In the final chapters, we'll explore more aspects of digital marketing, including customer loyalty, future trends, and staying ahead of the competition in the ever-evolving digital landscape.

11. Building Customer Loyalty and Retention

In the dynamic world of digital marketing, it's essential to not only acquire new customers but also to nurture existing ones.

This chapter focuses on strategies to build customer loyalty and improve retention rates for your small business.

Email Marketing for Customer Retention

Email marketing serves as a powerful tool not only for acquiring new customers but also for retaining and nurturing existing ones. Let's explore some advanced strategies for customer retention through email marketing, including customer segmentation, personalised recommendations, and leveraging your customers' feedback.

Customer Segmentation: Explore advanced segmentation techniques to tailor your email marketing campaigns to specific customer segments. Move beyond basic demographic segmentation and delve into behavioural and transactional segmentation.

Analyse customer behaviour, preferences, and purchase history to categorise them into segments with shared characteristics. For example, segment customers who frequently make purchases, those who engage with specific product categories, or those who have lapsed in activity.

By understanding the unique attributes of each segment, you can craft targeted and relevant email messages. This personalised approach enhances customer engagement and increases the likelihood of conversion.

Utilise automation tools to streamline the segmentation process and deliver timely, customised content that resonates with each segment. For example, online tools such as Mailchimp or Klaviyo can help to set up email sequences and automations efficiently.

Personalised Recommendations: Use email marketing as a platform for providing personalised product recommendations and exclusive offers to your loyal customers. Leverage customer data to understand their preferences and past purchases. Implement recommendation algorithms to suggest products or services that align with each customer's individual tastes. It sounds complicated but by using the right online tools and software it can be very simple.

Send personalised emails featuring these recommendations, creating a sense of exclusivity and personalised attention. Highlight new arrivals, complementary products, or items related to previous purchases.

By tailoring recommendations based on customer behaviour, you enhance the relevance of your email content, ultimately driving customer satisfaction and loyalty. Personalisation not only boosts sales but also strengthens the emotional connection between your brand and your customers.

Customer Feedback and Surveys: Harness the power of email marketing to gather valuable customer feedback through surveys. Develop strategies to understand customer satisfaction, preferences, and areas for improvement.

Craft well-designed surveys that encourage participation and provide actionable insights. Use these surveys to ask about product experiences, customer service interactions, or overall satisfaction with your brand. Incorporate open-ended questions to capture qualitative feedback.

Once collected, analyse the survey data to identify patterns and areas of concern. Utilise this feedback to make informed decisions on product enhancements, service improvements, or adjustments to your overall customer experience.

Demonstrating that you value customer opinions and actively seek their input not only enhances the customer-company relationship but also fosters a sense of community and collaboration.

When used well, email marketing for customer retention goes beyond generic campaigns. By implementing advanced segmentation, personalised recommendations, and leveraging customer feedback, businesses can create a customer-centric email strategy that not only retains customers but also strengthens their loyalty and engagement with the brand.

Social Media Engagement Strategies

Effective social media engagement is a cornerstone of building a vibrant online community and fostering lasting connections with your audience. This section explores key strategies for enhancing social media engagement, including creating engaging content, providing responsive customer service, and leveraging exclusive offers and promotions.

Engaging Content: Create social media content that not only informs but also encourages interactions and conversations with your followers. Understand the power of various engagement-focused content formats such as polls, quizzes, and contests.

Polls are an excellent way to involve your audience in decision-making or to gather opinions on specific topics. Quizzes add an element of interactivity and entertainment, allowing followers to participate and share their results. Contests, whether photo contests, caption contests, or giveaways, stimulate excitement and encourage user-generated content.

By fostering a two-way conversation through these engagement tools, you not only boost interaction but also increase the visibility of your content as engaged users share their participation with their networks – a vital part of growing your businesses digital presence.

Customer Service on Social Media: Explore the importance of providing responsive customer service on social media platforms. Social media is not only a broadcasting channel but also a direct avenue for customer inquiries and concerns.

Addressing customer inquiries promptly and effectively is crucial for maintaining a positive brand image. Discuss strategies for effective customer service on social media, including establishing response protocols, employing chatbots for immediate assistance, and ensuring consistent messaging.

Utilise social listening tools (such as orlo.tech or brandmentions.com) to monitor mentions and comments, allowing you to identify and address customer issues swiftly. By treating social media as an extension of your customer service channels, you demonstrate a commitment to customer satisfaction and build trust among your audience.

Exclusive Offers and Promotions: Leverage social media as a platform for providing exclusive offers and promotions to your loyal followers. Reward their continued engagement by offering special discounts, early access to sales, or exclusive promotions.

Create a sense of exclusivity and appreciation for your social media community. Whether it's a limited-time discount code, a flash sale, or a social media-exclusive giveaway, these promotions not only drive immediate engagement but also contribute to a sense of community and brand loyalty.

Encourage followers to share these exclusive offers, expanding your reach and attracting new audience members who want to be part of the exclusive perks.

Reward Programs and Customer Feedback

Building a strong foundation for customer loyalty involves implementing effective reward programs and leveraging valuable customer feedback. Let's look at the development of loyalty programs, strategies for soliciting customer feedback, and the continuous improvement processes that stem from customer insights.

Loyalty Programs: Developing customer loyalty programs is a strategic approach to incentivising repeat purchases and fostering long-term relationships. Design point-based systems, tiered rewards, and other incentives that resonate with your customer base.

Point-based systems allow customers to accumulate points with each purchase, which can then be redeemed for discounts, exclusive products, or other perks. Tiered rewards create a sense of progression, offering more significant benefits to customers who reach higher loyalty tiers. By understanding your customer's preferences and motivations, you can tailor your loyalty program to align with their expectations, driving increased engagement and repeat business.

Soliciting Customer Feedback: Encourage customers to leave reviews and provide feedback to gain valuable insights into their experiences with your products or services. Understand the impact of online reviews on your business's reputation and how to manage and respond to them.

Actively seek feedback through various channels, including email surveys, social media, and dedicated review platforms. Utilise incentives, such as discounts or exclusive access, to motivate customers to share their opinions.

Positive reviews can serve as powerful testimonials, influencing potential customers' perceptions, while negative reviews provide opportunities for improvement. Embrace customer feedback as a constructive tool that not only gauges satisfaction but also fosters a transparent and communicative relationship between your brand and its customers.

Always respond promptly to reviews online, especially negative reviews. It is very possible that addressing issues quickly can salvage your relationship with a dissatisfied customer, even converting some of them to be your most loyal and satisfied following! It also demonstrates to other viewers that you are keen to take feedback on board and improve the customer experience.

Continuous Improvement: Use customer feedback as a catalyst for continuous improvement across your products, services, and overall customer experience. Understand the value of feedback not only in identifying areas of concern but also in recognising strengths that can be further emphasised.

Analyse feedback systematically, categorising it based on themes or commonalities. Implement changes and enhancements based on this analysis to address customer pain points and enhance positive experiences. Demonstrating a commitment to continuous improvement not only increases customer satisfaction but also fosters brand loyalty.

Communicate improvements transparently to your customer base, showing that their feedback is valued and directly contributes to positive changes. This iterative process not only enhances your offerings but also reinforces the perception that your brand is responsive and customer-centric.

By providing incentives, actively seeking feedback, and making continuous improvements based on customer insights, your business can build stronger, more enduring relationships with your customers.

Chapter Summary

Building and maintaining customer loyalty is a critical component of your digital marketing strategy. By using email marketing for customer retention, implementing social media engagement strategies, and creating loyalty programs that reward customer loyalty and feedback, you can foster lasting relationships with your audience.

In the final chapter, we'll continue to explore more digital marketing strategies, including the impact of future trends and staying ahead of the competition in the ever-changing digital landscape.

12. Future Trends in Small Business Digital Marketing

The digital marketing landscape is ever-evolving, and staying ahead of the curve is crucial for small businesses to remain competitive.

This chapter explores the emerging trends and technologies that are likely to shape the future of digital marketing for small businesses, and some that are already doing so.

Artificial Intelligence and Machine Learning

In the realm of small business digital marketing, harnessing the capabilities of artificial intelligence (AI) and machine learning (ML) is a transformative approach. In this section we explore the utilisation of AI and ML in delivering personalised experiences through AI-powered personalisation tools, chatbots, recommendation engines, and the predictive analytics that drive informed marketing strategies.

AI-Powered Personalisation: AI-powered personalisation leverages algorithms and data analysis to tailor content, recommendations, and interactions to individual customer preferences.

Chatbots use natural language processing and machine learning to engage customers in real-time conversations. Chatbots enhance customer support, answer queries, and provide personalised recommendations, creating a seamless and interactive experience.

Dive into recommendation engines that use AI to analyse customer behaviour, predicting their preferences and suggesting relevant products or content. Content personalisation involves dynamically adapting website content, emails, or marketing messages based on user behaviour, enhancing engagement and conversion rates.

By embracing AI-powered personalisation, your small business can create a more engaging and tailored digital experience that resonates with your audience.

Predictive Analytics: Predictive analytics utilises AI and machine learning algorithms to analyse historical data and forecast future customer behaviour. Small businesses can leverage predictive analytics to identify trends, anticipate customer needs, and tailor marketing strategies accordingly. For instance, predictive analytics can help forecast which products or services are likely to be popular, allowing businesses to optimize inventory and marketing campaigns.

Additionally, it aids in customer segmentation, enabling targeted marketing efforts. Uncover the power of predictive lead scoring, where AI assesses the likelihood of a lead converting into a customer based on various factors.

By integrating predictive analytics using tools such as Microsoft Azure, into marketing decision-making, small businesses can make data-driven choices, optimise resource allocation, and stay ahead of evolving market trends.

.

Voice Search and Voice Assistants

The rise of voice search and the widespread adoption of voice-activated devices present unique opportunities for small businesses to enhance their online presence and tap into the emerging realm of voice commerce.

Voice Search Optimization: It is not discussed often enough but it is important for small businesses to recognise the growing importance of voice search as consumers increasingly turn to voice-activated devices like Apple's Siri, Amazon's Alexa and Google Assistant.

Voice search optimisation is crucial for ensuring that small businesses remain visible and accessible in this evolving landscape. Understand the nuances of conversational queries and long-tail keywords, as voice searches often mimic natural language.

Tailor your website content and SEO strategies to align with these conversational patterns, optimising for questions and contextually relevant information. Embrace local SEO, as voice searches often have a local intent. Ensuring accurate business information on platforms like Google My Business becomes paramount. By adapting to the rise of voice search, small businesses can position themselves as accessible and relevant in the expanding world of voice-activated technology.

Voice Commerce: Explore the potential of voice commerce and how your small business can integrate voice-activated sales and services into its operations. Voice commerce refers to the use of voice-activated devices for making purchases, accessing information, or interacting with brands.

Understand the consumer behaviours driving voice commerce, such as the convenience of hands-free interactions and the seamless nature of voice-activated transactions. Consider implementing voice-activated sales and services, allowing customers to place orders, make reservations, or access product information through voice commands.

Integrate secure and user-friendly voice payment options to facilitate transactions. As voice commerce continues to evolve, small businesses can leverage this technology not only to streamline customer interactions but also to stay at the forefront of consumer trends.

By adapting to the preferences of voice-activated device users and embracing the potential of voice commerce, small businesses can enhance their online visibility and provide seamless, innovative experiences for their customers.

Video Marketing and Live Streaming

In the realm of digital marketing, video content has emerged as a dominant force, offering small businesses unprecedented opportunities for brand visibility and audience engagement. Let's talk about insights into leveraging platforms like TikTok, YouTube and exploring interactive and shoppable video content.

Video Content Dominance:

Recognise the ongoing ascendancy of video marketing and its pivotal role in capturing audience attention.

Small businesses can harness the power of video to convey their brand story, showcase products or services, and establish a more personal connection with their audience. Platforms like YouTube provide a vast landscape for hosting and sharing video content, enabling businesses to reach a global audience.

TikTok is becoming more influential for small businesses, with the development of ads, Tiktok Shop and a move towards longer form content that will build in mid-video ads in the same way that YouTube has, creating a greater opportunity for businesses to advertise on the platform and reach vast or targeted audiences.

Understanding the nuances of each platform and tailoring content to align with the preferences of the target audience is essential.

Live streaming on social media platforms amplifies this engagement by offering real-time interactions. Whether it's behind-the-scenes glimpses, product launches, or Q&A sessions, live streaming fosters a sense of immediacy, encouraging audience participation. Small businesses can use live streaming to humanise their brand, build trust, and create memorable experiences for their audience.

By embracing these video-centric strategies, small businesses can carve out a compelling digital presence in an era where visual content is paramount.

Interactive Video:

Delve into the realm of interactive and shoppable video content, elevating audience engagement to new heights. Interactive videos empower viewers to actively participate in the content, whether through clickable elements, polls, or immersive storytelling experiences.

Small businesses can use interactive videos to create captivating narratives, gather feedback, and tailor content based on viewer preferences. This not only enhances engagement but also provides valuable insights into audience behaviour.

Shoppable videos take the interactive experience a step further, seamlessly integrating e-commerce functionality within the video content. Viewers can click on products showcased in the video and make purchases directly, creating a streamlined and frictionless shopping experience.

This innovative approach to video marketing aligns with the evolving expectations of digital consumers who seek a seamless transition from content consumption to action.

Video marketing and live streaming represent dynamic avenues for small businesses to enhance brand visibility and engage their audience effectively. By strategically leveraging platforms like YouTube and TikTok, embracing live streaming for real-time interactions, and exploring interactive and shoppable video content, small businesses can not only navigate the digital landscape but also stay at the forefront of evolving consumer preferences.

In an era where visual content reigns supreme, the incorporation of video strategies becomes a vital component of a comprehensive digital marketing strategy.

Influencer Marketing and User-Generated Content

In the ever-evolving landscape of digital marketing, influencer collaborations and user-generated content (UGC) have become powerful strategies for small businesses seeking authentic engagement and expanded reach and they are vital aspects to consider in your digital marketing strategy now.

Influencer Collaborations:

Discover the art of collaborating with influencers, especially micro-influencers, to create genuine and relatable content. Unlike macro-influencers, micro-influencers often have a more niche and engaged audience, making their endorsements resonate on a personal level. Small businesses can identify influencers whose values align with their brand and product offerings. Collaborating with influencers involves fostering authentic relationships, allowing them creative freedom to showcase products or services in an organic and relatable manner.

Moreover, small businesses can tap into their own pool of loyal customers to generate authentic user-generated content. Encourage customers to share their experiences, unboxing moments, or creative use of products on social media. This not only provides a genuine portrayal of the brand but also strengthens the connection with existing customers and attracts potential ones. By leveraging the influence of both external influencers and internal brand advocates, small businesses can amplify their online presence and foster a community around their products or services.

Social Commerce:

Dive into the phenomenon of social commerce, where the lines between social media and e-commerce blur, offering seamless shopping experiences directly on social platforms. With the rise of features like TikTok Shop and Facebook Marketplace, small businesses can integrate their product catalogue directly into social media profiles, streamlining the customer's journey from discovery to purchase. Explore the potential of shoppable posts and stories, where users can click on featured products and make purchases without leaving the platform.

By embracing social commerce, small businesses not only cater to the preferences of consumers who increasingly seek convenience but also tap into the social nature of online shopping. Encourage customers to share their purchases, provide reviews, and even create user-generated content showcasing how they use the products. This user-generated content, when integrated into social commerce strategies, adds authenticity and peer influence to the shopping experience, fostering a sense of community around the brand.

Influencer marketing and user-generated content stand as dynamic pillars in small business digital marketing. Through strategic collaborations with influencers, both external and internal, and harnessing the potential of social commerce, small businesses can forge meaningful connections with their audience, foster brand loyalty, and ultimately drive conversions.

These strategies not only capitalise on the authenticity that users seek but also align with the evolving landscape of social media as a comprehensive shopping destination. I honestly believe that small businesses need to embrace these aspects of marketing with gusto in 2024 to avoid being left behind!

Sustainability and Ethical Marketing

Sustainable Practices:

Embracing sustainability in digital marketing is not just an ethical choice but also a strategic move for small businesses aiming to build a positive brand image. Small businesses can integrate sustainable practices into their marketing strategies by highlighting eco-friendly initiatives, sourcing responsibly, and minimising environmental impact. Communicate these efforts through various channels, such as social media, email newsletters, and dedicated sections on the website, creating transparency and showcasing the commitment to sustainable practices.

Leveraging your eco-friendly practices extends beyond product manufacturing to packaging and shipping. Small businesses can opt for recyclable or biodegradable packaging materials, reducing the environmental footprint of their products. Communicating these choices to consumers not only fosters goodwill but also appeals to the growing segment of environmentally conscious customers. By incorporating sustainability into their marketing narrative, small businesses can differentiate themselves in the market, attract environmentally aware consumers, and contribute to a positive impact on the planet.

Moreover, small businesses can consider partnerships with environmental organisations, engage in community projects, or participate in initiatives that align with their sustainability goals. Collaborating on environmental initiatives not only demonstrates commitment but also provides opportunities for positive media coverage, further enhancing your brand's reputation.

Ethical Marketing:

Ethical marketing is also a cornerstone for building trust and fostering long-term relationships. Small businesses can prioritise transparency in their marketing messages, providing clear and honest information about their products, sourcing practices, and business operations. This transparency builds credibility and resonates with consumers who value openness and authenticity.

Corporate responsibility is another key aspect of ethical marketing. Small businesses can showcase their commitment to ethical practices by supporting social causes, ensuring fair employment and labour practices throughout your supply chain, and adhering to ethical production standards. By aligning marketing messages with a strong sense of ethics and responsibility, small businesses not only attract socially conscious consumers but also contribute to positive societal change.

Furthermore, ethical marketing involves avoiding deceptive practices, such as misleading claims or greenwashing. Clearly communicate the value of products or services without exaggeration and ensure that marketing materials accurately represent your brand's commitments. Small businesses that prioritise ethical marketing build a loyal customer base, as consumers increasingly seek brands that align with their values.

Integrating sustainable practices and adopting ethical marketing strategies are not only ethical imperatives but also smart business moves for small businesses. By showcasing your commitment to sustainability, minimising your environmental impact, and prioritising ethical marketing, your small business can differentiate itself, attract socially conscious consumers, and contribute to a positive impact on both the environment and society. These efforts not only build a strong brand reputation but also position small businesses as responsible contributors to a more sustainable and ethical business landscape.

Augmented Reality (AR) and Virtual Reality (VR)

AR Marketing:

Augmented Reality (AR) opens up exciting possibilities for small businesses to create immersive and interactive advertising experiences that captivate their audience. AR overlays digital content onto the real-world environment, providing users with an enhanced, interactive view of their surroundings.

As a small business you can leverage AR in various ways, such as creating AR filters for social media platforms, enabling customers to virtually try on products or visualise how certain items look in their own spaces.

One practical application of AR marketing is in the beauty and fashion industry, where customers can use AR filters to see how different makeup products or clothing items look on themselves before making a purchase. Additionally, AR can enhance print materials like brochures or business cards, allowing customers to scan them with a mobile device to unlock interactive content, special promotions, or 3D product demonstrations.

By incorporating AR into their marketing strategies, small businesses not only provide a unique and engaging experience but also showcase innovation, a great way to set your business apart in the competitive digital landscape.

VR for Product Visualisation:

Virtual Reality (VR) takes the concept of immersive experiences to the next level, and for small businesses, it offers a powerful tool for product visualisation and creating virtual showrooms. VR enables customers to step into a virtual environment where they can explore products in three dimensions, almost as if they were physically present. This is particularly beneficial for businesses selling large or customisable items, such as furniture or interior design services.

Small businesses can develop virtual showrooms that allow customers to experience products in a simulated space. For example, a furniture store could create a VR showroom where customers can virtually arrange and visualise different pieces of furniture in their homes before making a purchase. This not only enhances the customer's shopping experience but also reduces the need for physical showrooms, making it a cost-effective solution for small businesses with limited resources.

Moreover, VR can be used for educational and training purposes. Small businesses can create immersive training programs or virtual tours to showcase their operations, manufacturing processes, or behind-the-scenes glimpses, fostering a deeper connection with their audience.

By embracing VR for product visualisation, your small business can provide a futuristic and highly engaging way for customers to interact with your offerings, ultimately enhancing the overall brand experience.

Data Privacy and Compliance

Data Protection:

In the context of UK legislation (other countries have different legislation but much will follow the same principles), data protection primarily revolves around compliance with the General Data Protection Regulation (GDPR). GDPR is a comprehensive set of regulations designed to protect the privacy and personal data of individuals within the European Union (EU), including the UK. For small businesses operating in the UK, adherence to GDPR is crucial. This is a piece of legislation that was adapted and retained in the UK following Brexit.

GDPR mandates that businesses handle personal data responsibly and transparently. This includes obtaining explicit consent from individuals before collecting their data, clearly stating the purpose of data collection, and ensuring the security and confidentiality of the data. Small businesses must implement robust data protection measures, such as encryption and secure storage, to safeguard personal information from unauthorised access or breaches.

Additionally, GDPR grants individuals certain rights over their data, such as the right to access, rectify, and erase their information. Small businesses need to establish processes to address these rights promptly. Non-compliance with GDPR can result in significant fines, making it imperative for small businesses to stay informed about evolving data protection regulations and continuously adapt their practices to remain in compliance.

If you use individuals' data in your small business you will need to be registered with the Information Commissioner's Office (ICO) which incurs a fee – the fee depends on the size of you business but for most small businesses it is a low fee.

Consumer Trust and Transparency:

Consumer trust is a cornerstone of successful business relationships, and in the digital age, transparency in data collection and handling plays a pivotal role in establishing and maintaining that trust. Small businesses must be transparent about how they collect, use, and store customer data. This involves providing clear and easily accessible privacy policies that outline the purpose of data collection, the types of data collected, and how that data will be used.

Transparency also extends to informing customers about any third parties with whom their data may be shared. If small businesses utilise cookies on their websites, they should inform users and provide options for cookie preferences clearly. This not only ensures compliance with regulations but also fosters a sense of control and understanding for consumers.

Building consumer trust through transparency involves being open about data security measures in place to protect against unauthorised access. Small businesses should communicate their commitment to data protection and outline the steps taken to secure customer information. By establishing a culture of transparency, small businesses can differentiate themselves in a crowded market and build long-term relationships with customers who feel confident in the responsible handling of their data.

Chapter Summary

Embracing these current and emerging trends in digital marketing is essential for small businesses to remain competitive in the evolving digital landscape. By staying informed and adapting to new technologies and customer expectations, small businesses can position themselves for success in the future of digital marketing.

13. Conclusion

Congratulations on completing your journey through the world of small business digital marketing! This comprehensive guide has provided you with the knowledge, strategies, and insights to effectively navigate the ever- evolving digital landscape and promote your small business successfully online.

In the next few pages we'll reflect on some of the key takeaways that you should bear in mind as you continue on your small business marketing journey.

Recap of Key Takeaways

Some of the key takeaways from our exploration of digital marketing that you may want to have a real focus on include:

Understanding Your Audience: Your target audience is at the core of your digital marketing efforts. Knowing them well and catering to their needs is fundamental. Detailed customer personas are a must have!

Digital Presence: Building a strong online presence, including a professional website, engaging content, and active social media profiles on the platforms that are right for your small business, is the foundation of successful digital marketing.

Multifaceted Approach: Digital marketing is not a one-size-fits-all strategy. Utilising various channels such as SEO, PPC, email marketing, social media, and content marketing provides a holistic approach to reaching your audience.

Data-Driven Decisions: Data is invaluable in digital marketing. Using analytics and performance data to make informed decisions is a recurring theme throughout this book for a reason!

Customer Loyalty: It's not just about acquiring customers; building loyalty and retaining existing ones are equally important. Customer feedback, personalised experiences, and loyalty programs play a significant role.

Adaptation to Current & Future Trends: The digital marketing landscape is ever-evolving. Staying ahead of current and emerging trends such as AI, voice search, video marketing, influencer collaborations, and sustainability is crucial. Give serious consideration to this in 2024 and if you are not already on TikTok for your business think about it seriously!

You don't have to be perfect at everything you try first time – taking action, being prepared to make mistakes and learn from them is the first step on the way to success!

Your Path to Success

Speaking of the way to success, as you move forward in your digital marketing journey, remember that success doesn't happen overnight. It's the result of consistent effort, learning from your experiences, and staying open to innovation. Here are some parting tips to guide you:

Stay Informed: Keep up with the latest developments in digital marketing by reading industry blogs, attending webinars, and joining relevant communities.

Experiment and Learn: Don't be afraid to try new strategies and test different approaches. Learning from your successes and failures is key to growth.

Consistency is Key: Whether it's posting regular content, engaging on social media, or maintaining email campaigns, consistency is vital for building trust and loyalty.

Customer-Centric Approach: Always put your customers at the forefront of your decisions. Understand their needs and tailor your marketing efforts accordingly.

Data-Driven Optimisation: Continually analyse your data and adapt your strategies to improve performance. What works today may not work tomorrow.

Adapt and Evolve: Be prepared to adapt to changing market conditions and consumer behaviours. The ability to pivot and innovate is a hallmark of successful businesses.

Your Journey Continues

Your journey in the world of digital marketing doesn't end here. It's a continuous process of learning, adapting, and growing. As the digital landscape evolves, so will your strategies and approaches. Embrace the ever-changing nature of digital marketing, and you'll be well-equipped to achieve your small business's long-term success in the digital age.

Thank you for joining me on this journey through "The Small Business Digital Marketing Playbook." I really wish you the best of luck in all your digital marketing endeavours, and am excited to see your small business thrive in the digital world.

With this, The Small Business Digital Marketing Playbook now complete. If you have any additional questions or need further assistance, feel free to email me jemma@jemmavwright.com.

Good luck with your digital marketing efforts!

Printed in Great Britain
by Amazon